Comb

Shadab Zeest Hashmi

Cover and interior design by Daniel Krawiec
Cover and interior art by Salma Ahmad Caller

ISBN 978-1-7333671-3-4
Second Edition

Sable Books
sablebooks.org

Contents

For my Father

"Owl's soft hoot in the Hanging Gardens of Babylon.
A cold wind blows scraggly bits of history east of the Khyber Pass."

— Sohrab Sepehri

"I am frightened
of my language, of the air combing a willow, frightened
of the clarity of dense time..."

— Mahmoud Darwish

Comb

One breath away from invasion, one page away from a new chapter of empire, Peshawar, the city with an open door— the *baab e Khyber*— for a symbol, houses a guard in its heart.

As a final threshold of the corridor between pursuers of power from the East and West, its location is a curse. Being history's blank preface, inked by empire again and again, its guard is perpetual no matter who enters.

It is my hometown.

And it was as the Soviet War began across the border in Afghanistan, and chaos bubbled up invisibly, erupting from an overheard sentence or caught in a suspicious silence, or in flashes from the seven o'clock news that froze in my head, that I could no longer wake up without stomach pain.

It was then that the breaking of combs began.

Cardiff by the Sea

My hair smells of seaweed.

Wave after opalescent wave, my feet are boring through drenched Pacific sand, molding it into two shapeless urns. I have the sudden urge to dislodge and run away. Neither the ocean's unreeling nor its refrain of explosions will resolve. I am twenty-three, just married, bewildered at being suddenly halved and doubled.

The ocean shimmers like so much spilled soda, as a poet once said. Who am I in this land of abundance? A beachcomber may find in my shin-deep urns what I haven't yet found: my essence.

In essence, I may be:
a languid flamingo
an ancient copper samovar
a flautist's breath
an elk draped with an heirloom sari
a cobalt and yellow balustrade
a trapeze rope
a turtle singing to seven generations of offspring
a spindle whorl wound with miles of Ikat silk
a diacritic stroke on a Sufi's coffee-stained page

Wait.
Don't wait.
There will be no occasion to explore my essence. Many years from now, while presenting at a Literature Festival in North Carolina, someone will ask about how or how much I share my spiritual quest in my work. My answer: Is there a choice but to write in empire's language, language in which I'm forever a lurking shadow? One can only write about God if one comes to own words.

From the cusp dividing countries and tongues, and from the cusp of divided selves, I write.

Ghosts of a Frontier City

A single feather, milky blue, just fallen on my threshold, is from a Turkestan hill dove flying south from China to Peshawar, I imagine, though it is more likely to have been shed by a buttonquail which is common in these parts.

There is no house or door, only a threshold with the listening capacity of a mystic; there is unstoppable song and news in the hubbub. My impatience will keep me from staying by the threshold. I'll fly over it like a bird from India or Afghanistan, or I'll cross back and forth like local ants and lizards, run by the small animal clock inside me.

When I migrate, something of the threshold will migrate with me.

Made from melting the musk of each passerby with protolithic time, this threshold is neither a construction nor a destruction but a slow composite of both. Along the Silk Road— the moving marketplace across Asia, parts of Africa and Europe— Peshawar has been an important outpost: here, what is stolen by opium, is filled back in by shady trees planted by pilgrims; what is healed and made whole with medicinal tea and Sufi poetry, is pulverized by gun powder; there are rare gems and there are bullets. Sometimes trade and war ride each other's shoulders. A third companion, the storyteller, is often a few paces ahead or behind.

Qissa Khawani Bazaar or "the market of the storytellers" has teashops where traders, craftsmen, monks, poets, warriors, spies, scholars, pilgrims, thieves and builders traveling the Silk Road, have, for long, gathered to exchange stories.

But some stories tell themselves, like the story of the old Banyan tree chained by James Squid, a British military officer who got this tree in the Landi Kotal Cantonment "arrested" for lurching at him on a very drunken night: the punished tree's shame is intensified by its caption "I am under arrest." The tree is locked in history as is the British Raj's moment of inebriation with power.

Not far from Peshawar's military areas are the two unforgettable libraries of my childhood— the British Council with its air conditioned, brusque smell and the soothing secret of a raised reading nook, an antechamber with round cane stools for children— and the Peshawar Club library where there sits on the shelf, a shadow book for every book; every footfall and turning of the page is heard by ardent colonial ghosts.

In the other environs of this ancient city, the ruins, stupas, temples, orchards, caravanserais, graveyards, *havelis*, universities and forts, there are ghosts of other inhabitants: Persians, Greeks, Hindus, Buddhists, Marathas, Mughals, Afghans, Sikhs. Peshawar has been the heart of the Gandhara civilization, beloved "Lotus Land" for Kushan kings, its "Pipal Mandi" known for the sacred Pipala (Bodhi tree) under which Buddha is said to have preached.

A city of many names throughout history, Peshawar's modern name, consonant with Purushapura, one of its ancient names, is said to have been the coinage of the Mughal emperor Akbar in the sixteenth century. Peshawar means "the one that comes before," or the frontier. The first Mughal Babur's remarks upon entering the subcontinent through here, are not flattering— it is dull compared to his verdant home Ferghana in southern Central Asia. The Mughal emperors would fill it with gardens, dubbing Peshawar "the city of flowers" and leave, among other treasures, a beautiful seventeenth century mosque.

Legend has it that Khizer— the green-robed saint who appears to people who are lost and trying to find their way— comes to this Mughal mosque to pray. The mosque, Masjid Mahabat Khan, is bathed in elegant carnelian and ivory colors and surrounded by shop fronts of goldsmiths and jewelers who claim that this sacred place is befitting for their trade of precious goods. The faithful have been called to prayer five times a day for hundreds of years but there are chilling memories of other days, of the accused being hurled from the top of the minaret in summary executions carried out by the Italian mercenary and governor of Peshawar under Sikh rule, Paolo Avitabile— a tyrannical figure who has entered folklore as Abu Tabela.

Besides the well-known Khyber Pass, there is another passage here that has shaped global history; it is an ancient highway connecting the subcontinent with central Asia. Called *"Uttarapath"* in Maurian times, it was rebuilt and modernized by the Bihar-born Pathan king Sher Shah Suri. The road, *"Sarrak e Azam"* (the "Great Road") or *"Badshahi Sarrak"* (the "Royal Road")— extends from Kabul to Bengal, an engineering feat of the sixteenth century— was renovated and renamed the "Grand Trunk Road" by the British. A multitude of cultures jostle each other along this road—Muslim, Sikh, Christian, Hindu, Parsi, Buddhist and others; it links the regions of present-day Afghanistan, Pakistan, India, and Bangladesh. In Peshawar, part of this road is still named Jamrud and a footbridge over it is a thoroughfare for students walking to and from a complex of colleges in the area; part of it is tree-lined, part arid— the Safed Koh mountains visible in the distance.

The city smells of bus fumes and is heartbreakingly resplendent in springtime— there are richly fragrant apricots and melons. The elderly men and women are thought precious and receive a kind of reverence that sweetens the air.

The Sikh fort, Mughal marketplace, British clock tower, modern hotels and shopping plazas, cinemas, stadiums are astir with life.

Since the time of the Soviet War, I have seen these places in the aftermath of bomb blasts. I have seen the insult of human flesh exploding into lifeless ribbons hanging from lampposts. I have heard children and birds shrieking in panic.

In the register of shattering glass lives protolithic time, chipping away, accruing. Nothing goes unrecorded, unwoven. With each passerby, the mulberry curtain exhales, hanging over the threshold, the frontier.

Broken Comb

On our way to the smugglers' market:
I'm drawing the shapes of hairclips I want, and making a list
of colors:

Yellow (like loquat)
Blue-black (like the eye of a water buffalo)
Kashmiri-cream-tea pink

Important: need a new comb too, a stronger one (but with the
same spotted light brown handle that, when held up against
sunlight, shines with some old story world living within).

Every time I comb my hair, I like to place the comb on my
nose-bridge and look inside the sepia-lit plastic handle.

A stronger one this time.

Smugglers' Market

My little brother and I both rush to the car, still in our *chap-
pals*, as the driver is pulling out. Ami says yes, come, if homework is done. My big brother will stay at home and read
everything there is to read in his room, on the wood shelves,
on the glass shelves, the library.

The smuggler's market is a popular place, sells everything
from safety pins to refrigerators, apple-scented soaps, thermos flasks, crepe silk, organza, net or marina fabric, chewing gum, bone china, air conditioners. My first bike, a green
Soviet model, is from here.

Ilaqa ghair, the outskirts of the city where the law of the land
does not apply, deals in smuggled goods: no taxes or duties.

On the way back, there is a checkpoint where you declare the items you've bought.

When the uniformed men open the trunk and passenger door to check our shopping, a cold breeze enters, the car is usually filled with the aroma of warm chapli kababs. It's the precise aroma of being taken care of, to the core. I'll remember it with tears in my eyes when I go abroad to study.

Naan/Kabab with Cricket

Ami unties the thin white string around the Urdu newspaper that the bread (longer than my arm) is wrapped in, unfolds the bread to reveal the chapli kababs' charred exterior, fleck-ed with dried pomegranate seeds, red pepper flakes and to-matoes. The naan/kabab are hot and moist and humble and satiate hunger before and beyond intelligible hunger; a small piece of bread with kabab textured slightly crunchy on the outside, softened with eggs, onions and wheat flour, spiced with coriander— a morsel or "luqma" formed by my Ami's hands for my mouth— is how I know I have a share in the vast universe, that I'm part of its hunger and it is part of mine, that my mother is my bridge to the now and later, the here, the away, and maybe even the never or the forever, the great beyond which I'm meant to hunger for, the contours of a consciousness shaped and fed.

In Cricket season, Abi likes us to eat in the lounge instead of the dining room.

The game of Cricket stretches out time; it can claim ownership of hours and days at a time, in which span the screen loses all color except the green of the field, the dust colored pitch and the bobbing of the white uniforms that the cameras follow.

The sound of cricket commentary teaches me the timbre of collective emotion— tentative anticipation, surprise, thrill, disappointment, pride, celebration. The game with its colonial accents, players (with the multitude of skin tones of the commonwealth) wearing flared white pants, floppy hats, and cable-knit sweaters— native and foreign at the same time— is a surreal reenactment of history: the possibility, every time, of a winner from a different spot on the spectrum as opposed to the winning being the monochromatic privilege.

I don't have the patience for this game but I like its aura because it is my father's, though he doesn't play cricket, he plays squash at the Peshawar club where we go for lunch, library or family movie nights under the stars.

Peshawar club is a building from Raj times with high ceilings and thick, white walls; the movies they show on Friday nights are American. One movie, in particular, stays with me for long; it's called *Yeti*.

It's about a monster that lives in the Himalayas.

Chinese Acrobats at Peshawar Club

On an autumn night, starry and dewy and fairy-lit, I am squeezing Ami's hand, a habit of mine, as we take our seats on the lawn to watch an acrobatics show. I'm fascinated by her delicate sari, perfume, white gloves, and rings with which she lets me play until I drop one in the grass and manage to annoy her.

The troupe of Chinese acrobats is stunning. I'm especially impressed by the agility and strength of the female acrobats and I find that my eyes are not trained to follow motion so fast or to parse the visual language of arms, torsos, legs forming pedestals for others to stand on or hang from— I will grow up to learn that womanhood is exactly this: a feat of acrobatics, with proverbial lifting, boosting, connecting, carrying, but mostly bending—in innumerable ways—not spectacular or even visible, an apparatus with a secretly turbulent energy fueling the constant mechanics of multifarious demands. We are taught to bear with silence, taught that silence is grace and grace is a dialect of might.

And then there is the elaborate language of beauty with its myriad dialects, some used as rungs of hierarchy in an ever evolving game of power and oppression, and some map a personal, inwardly ennobling journey of the spirit, an affirmation and celebration of the swirling music and color of the cosmos itself.

I'm dazzled by the jeweled hair-knots of the female acrobats.

The Acrobat's Hairpin

is a landscape on a stick
precipice
in verawood
        color of meteor?   carrion crow?   wineberry?
                      Cascade
                          in fortune-green
                            agate
For every bit of steel in her gut
she carries
        an exquisitely
                  -lipped
                      plum
                        blossom
                          of spiraling
                      gold enamel
                on her head
            Boughs
      delicately
      rup-
      tured
blushing
with
tourmaline
flowers
and
a spray
      of coral
        pearl
buds   the   dark   river   of   her   spine

Nests

"That the birds of worry and care fly about your head, this you cannot change, but that they build nests in your hair, this you can prevent," says a Chinese proverb.

My hair becomes a nesting place for worries I have yet to name. The hum of nest-makers is incessant; I make the mistake of tuning in to them, rather, I make the mistake of forming a habit of it. There must be a million species of worry-birds circling for a chance to settle in my hair. The first of these is the increasing awareness of vulnerability.

Our lounge, with a door leading to my room, another to the lawn, another to the kitchen, another to our parents' bedroom, is the ultimate nest. This is where we race, sitting on small stools, or take turns in my feeding chair that has been ingeniously repurposed by Bhai, my older brother, into a swing hung on the bannister of the staircase, or have meals if there is cricket going on, where we have daily fights with Ami over having to drink milk after homework, or where we test the Quran teacher's patience as he settles in a butterfly shaped chair to teach us Arabic pronunciation, where Bhai raises his arms in the *bhangra* pose and we all indulge in a stealthy *bhangra* dance as soon as *maulvi sahib's* back is turned; it is where we watch occasional Tom & Jerry or Popeye cartoons or have treats of bonbon biscuits or pistachio-honey nougat that Abi brings from his trips to Karachi.

One day the doors of the lounge that lead to all the important places of my tiny world, teach me not to trust them, that a door is not entirely a safe, predictable or accessible thing, that every enterprise, every relationship, every moment in history has a door. One can get locked in or out.

This happens in the first and most frightful nightmare of my childhood.

The creature with a wild mane

It's early afternoon, I'm in a small, orange plastic tub, playing with water. I have a vague sense that my brothers are around, playing in the yard, Ami goes inside every now and then but even when inside she can watch me from the kitchen window. Then, suddenly, it's nightfall and I'm alone.

I can see lights in the windows but the door is closed. I cannot believe I was left alone.

It gets colder. The stars are bright and roll around like billiard balls. A head rises from behind the wall. It is the lion-man of my brother's woolen sweater:

the knitted creature/ with a fixed gaze/
and a wild lion mane

I'm trapped between a locked door and the terrible gaze of a creature with a mane of brown yarn.

Nothing about this chilling scene will ever be easy to forget, though right here, on this lawn, the best memories are yet to come.

Hairspray at the PTV Station

What they do not understand at the PTV station is that it's in my nature to be elsewhere, nodding attentively one minute, gone the next. I don't understand it either, the tendency to let myself be stolen into another world, switching between here and there like flashes of moon jellies, now lit, now dim. I am six and always behind by a few moments or hours even in the sleepy town of Peshawar with its gray mountain-scape, *chinar* trees and flaxen afternoons; its rhythms defined less by blasting horns of public buses, or noise of plaza construction, more by the *Mochi*, the tap-tapping cobbler who could sew together anything from a ripped shoe buckle to a suitcase, the churning of the dyer with smoke rising from his boiling dyes and moist *dupatta* scarves in solids or tie-dye bellowing joyfully on a grid of ropes, or the radio playing commentary in cricket season, the sudden bursts and crescendos of the cheering crowds.

I'll forget the color and contours of the PTV building but remember vividly my obsession with skipping across large square tiles, instead of walking normally from the makeup room to the studio. The makeup artist is a friendly lady, who, it seems can't ever do her work without chewing gum. She smells like hairspray, lipstick and moist makeup foundation: the smells I love in this surreal, mirrored room, makeup being my favorite of all forbidden things.

In the producer's room Marie biscuits and blue-rimmed teacups with thick *chai* are in constant supply. I find myself mesmerized by the upside down reflection of *Quaid-e-Azam* Jinnah's photo on the glass top of the desk, dizzied by the reflected motion of the ceiling fan—all the while trying to memorize lines. The props are another distraction: how could I not tinker with larger than life butterflies and flowers?

Once, I eat up all the sweet *choori* meant for the parrot that is to appear on my show. When I am told they've designed a door in a large apple for me to make an entry from, for the upcoming recording, I am too excited to keep it a secret and tell everyone I know, weeks before the actual episode. In the days before video games and the internet, emerging out of an apple is terribly newsworthy.

When I "sign" a six-month contract for "Geeto Kahay Kahani", a television show for children, I, of course, don't really know what it entails. It takes me three weeks, with three rehearsals and what seemed like a million takes of recording each week (typically one long afternoon) to announce to my mother that I want to quit. I list all the discomforts: the studio lights make me hot, my clothes are itchy, I can't memorize the script, snacks are not allowed in the recording studio, "kids at school know that that girl on TV is me and they talk about me in the third person..." My producer, a gentleman who speaks with a thoughtful timbre, is distraught. The show is on national hook-up, and has made a successful debut.

The show runs for a year and a half, winning me celebrity among the four to ten-year-old TV-watching demographic, an award for being the youngest compere in the country and some special privileges like exemption from homework by teachers who actually watch "Geeto." I don't much like the show myself because the vocal ticks that the public finds endearing aren't something I am proud of, my artlessness not anything I personally fancy. Plus, I am convinced I have lost something in the process. I have no clue what it is.

It will only be after knowing myself as a writer, years after those illiterate days of prep and class-one in junior school, that I'll understand that this TV stint is a contradictory gift; serendipitous to a child of my inclinations, tuned into parallel worlds, and engaged in connecting them inwardly but blocked from any viable outlet because her public persona is of someone else's imagining.

It is certainly lucky to be exposed to the magic of a process that combines art, technology, a team of people synthesizing an illusion that comes off better than reality— all beyond my understanding but endlessly fascinating. I am able to appreciate the contrast between the seamlessness of the final product and the process with its fits and starts and inexplicable gaps which are partly due to the time it takes for the camera, sound and light people to synchronize, partly because of my idiosyncrasies such as watching myself on the monitor instead of looking at the camera, or, forgetting the script, or wolfing down the bird-food I am supposed to feed the parrot (my unwitting guest on the show).

I am not unlike that parrot as I confront a public response to my TV persona without having a language of my own to differentiate myself from my persona. The parrot however will not go through the anguish of desiring articulation, nor feel any urgency to describe the light in the studio bouncing off and splitting, the perfect silence of a fan-less room when the "On Air" sign is on, or what it's like to close one's eyes and hold one's breath just before the makeup lady presses the can of hairspray, chewing gum on her breath.

Shaping Ramadan

The fridge is between pesto and grasshopper green; the dining table is oval. A cubist picture hangs on the wall. It changes meaning, depending on the time of the day and the way I fall into its shapes and clever shades. The fish in the painting's octagon looks like a remote-control car or a scarf sometimes, then it goes back to being a fish; the face is sometimes benign, sometimes not. On a good day, this dining room has the aura of sweet cream, *parathay* (fried bread) and chilled mangoes, otherwise, cabbage and beets. There is a door that opens to the foyer; I'm as tall as the doorknob.

My seat at the dining table faces the window. Here is where I practice "joining handwriting" (what "cursive" is called in Pakistan), glancing, from time to time at Sadequain's Quranic calligraphy on the wall: a composition that has Arabic letters made to look like sailboats in which other letters nestle. It cools the room. As an adult there will be many reasons to recall this piece— its placid dignity, its nests of words from the holy book— in a world where my Muslim identity will know no sanctuary, no dignity, where verses from the book will be twisted, desecrated by fellow-Muslims, where large populations of Muslims will be punished by the enemy for the crimes of a few, or for no crime at all.

It is the month of Ramadan. I have many notebooks of summer homework to fill but the heat makes it hard to concentrate. I study the pattern of the tablecloth, the occasional lizard on the wall. The swinging door to the kitchen startles me every now and then as my brothers come running through it. They use motion to navigate the world, I, reverie. We balance each other's energies and are most in harmony in the loquat or guava season, or in Ramadan when the family bonds over *Iftaar*, the meal at sundown, typically consisting of dates, lemonade or lemon barley squash, mango milkshake, *pakoray* (chickpea fritters), spicy fruit salad, *samosay* and other snacks. There is a certain aroma associated with the fasting season, owing to this traditional menu. It is the aroma of festivity and fatigue, chatter and silent meditation.

At age seven, I insist on keeping my first Ramadan fast. I'm old enough to practice a bit of self-discipline, not old enough to appreciate the full meaning of fasting (that slight detail having to do with enhancing the spiritual life!). The day is immeasurably long. I stand by the window to watch the slow day wilt. I give my mother a (long and badly spelt) list of treats for *iftaar*. She cooks every single item and finds the misspelt list too amusing not to save for posterity. I add drawings to my menu: triangular *samosay*, coils of orange *jalaibi*, round *parathay*. It will be important for posterity to know the shapes and colors of Ramadan food, I imagine.

Steel Comb

I feel in the pit of my stomach the proximity to my school as the car approaches the Air Force base and the diminutive Air Force planes become visible on the runway through the large gates. The car would now turn into the school lane and another day, the stuff of nightmares, would begin for me with the stomach cramps known in Urdu as "twist in the stomach."

Ami tries to calm me down before school without much luck, though I'll forever remember how softly she speaks, saying I'm the bravest person she knows. I dress myself with painstaking care, making sure the *shalwar* doesn't lose its crease, the black shoes are spotlessly polished, the white PT ("Physical Training") shoes have been cleaned with white polish that has dried properly, without congealing.

My fingers are tense and my comb breaks into pieces; I would lose many over the years.

Finally, Ami buys me a steel comb.

My desire becomes a prayer on my lips
lab peh ati hai dua ban keh tammana meri

The daily assembly at P.A.F school starts with the Music Master leading an uninspired rendition of Iqbal's famous poem *"lab peh ati,"* a powerful lyric harnessing the classical metaphor of the devoted moth desiring the candle of knowledge; Iqbal's passionate verses warped into the whiney trill of children interested only in live experiments of their own vocal range, utterly oblivious to the poetry. The national anthem is sung, which, being mostly in "Urdu e mualla" (Persian diction), is beyond us Junior School students. In class five I would understand the anthem and admire the beauty of the words, and wonder why it had to be written in the high Urdu that no one understood, not that I would ever want to change the song; the clipped monosyllabic "qom," "mulk" swelling into a crescendo with the lofty "*sul-tan-at*," and drowning into the high note of "*Pa-inda ta-binda baad*" and then the decrescendo, the softening into a prayer "*shaad baad manzil-e-Murad*," roughly translated as "may you happily find your noble destiny" – a prayer like a broken thing, open in its cracks to let go of endless sadness— the sadness of an endlessly breaking people, a poem to hold them together. Stepping up to enter the complex beauty of the anthem is to understand that it embodies the intricate, seemingly inaccessible path the founding fathers set us upon, that to decode the poem is to find the seams between our past and future.

Dolly

I am in Prep A, the kindergarten room with the overwhelming aroma of French toast (Pakistani French toast is eggier and sweeter), and *Rooh Afza*, the super sweet, bright red herb drink in little chubby flasks. The smell comes from a mountain of lunch boxes in a corner that the *ayah* arranges and fusses over. Here, in this room I spend one whole year, and learn (besides ABCs and *Alif bay pay)*, from a stray comment by my teacher, that I am too fat to be selected for the role of "Dolly" in the class play to be performed at the annual function, and I must make my peace with the role of Miss Polly. I'm quite sure I'm average, neither fat nor thin. I suspect there is more to the teacher's comment, and that she uses "fat" as a euphemism for "not pretty enough;" Either way, at home I have plenty of reasons to believe I'm just fine and that life is a lot more than looks; I also know that though I prefer the role of Dolly to Miss Polly, it's not the end of the world to play Miss Polly. My shoulders learn to shrug.

As an only daughter in the house, growing up without sisters, girl-cousins, girl-friends, I don't have anyone to share notes with; I'll meet female protagonists mostly in my grandmother's stories, heroines of history such as Rabia Basri the Sufi, or Sultana Raziah the sovereign, or the Bronte sisters who create female characters of strength and sensitivity, some of them, such as Jane Eyre described as being of passable beauty.

Though the female figures I have come to know in life and in books are empowering images, my encounters with women through the years would teach me something different. The notion of female strength as an intellectual and spiritual cultivation would be challenged again and again. As an adult I'll become wary of being trapped into performing the feminine, a trap set in deadlier ways in the domain of women than the domain of men. The self-appointed judges and juries of my face, form, appearance, taste, as well as any accomplishments, or lack thereof, related to building a career or family life, would not be men but other women. I would cringe at comments designed to boost the speakers, about my earnings being less than theirs, their proverbial *chapatis* being rounder than mine or their bodies being skinnier than mine; a tribe, a "sisterhood" so desperate to feel superior that they would put down one of their own, is no tribe of mine, I'd decide. Somewhere between the noise of competitive "one-up-woman-ship," and the silencing from men, I'll learn to recognize the faint but deep articulation of true friendships coming from the few human beings who would help me see glimpses of what lies beyond the material, who would lead me to be a humble witness of Divine beauty, the only beauty that counts, the only beauty that counters the damage from the delusional theater of power.

Uniform Veil

Between the hanging of Bhutto and the beginning of Zia's regime, we wear the strangest uniform. Thus far, it was grey skirts and white blouses with gray blazers. In class one, a white *shalwar* is added to the skirt while the establishment is still in the process of considering how best to implement modesty in school life. Soon they settle on a grey *kameez* and a white *shalwar*, which makes me personally happy as I find skirts and frocks infantilizing; to wear anything seriously stylish such as your mother's wardrobe of *shalwar kameez*, *dupattas* and *saris*, you have to be old enough.

All eleven years I'll attend P.A.F, the boys wear the same grey pants, white shirts with ties, V-neck sweaters and blazers. Western attire is more appropriate because it seems more in keeping with the regimented military life that the school is a microcosm of; the rules for boys' haircut are severely strict for the same reason. Unpolished shoes, overgrown nails, and less than perfect hygiene are serious offenses for which one can be publicly shamed.

In senior school, the white sash over *shalwar kameez* is replaced by a narrow white veil or *dupatta*; in order to incorporate the change in an organized manner, a special assembly for girls is called and the Fine Arts teacher is asked to draw an illustration and demonstrate how to wear a veil as uniform, how to cover the hair neatly, pin the house badge to the left of the *kameez* collar, how to tuck the veil inside the blazer.

Pakistan in general, and Peshawar in particular, is a laid-back society, sleepy at all times, and I'm fascinated by the disjunction of the Air Force culture, its proper and properly robotic ways. Even the medical staff walk briskly in their crisp khaki outfits; women doctors in thick khaki *saris*, military badges pinned on the *pallu*. It is a curious thing that Pakistani Air Force doctors wear the *sari* as uniform.

Inverted Image

A beautifully kept campus with mature vegetation and neat flowerbeds, P.A.F is a well-run place where disciplinary actions became chilling legends. Because I do well in academics, I am made a prefect in class ninth and tenth; a cop, a cog in the wheel of this stressful environment, making sure no one deviates from the rules. Chewing gum, wearing nail polish, not staying in single file, and many other trivial things are to be reported. Life is without joy and I have been rewarded for being a good student by being welcomed into the establishment as an enforcer of sorts, along with select others who earn top marks.

As a science student, I am briefly happy watching colorful fumes, inverted images and brainless, spineless life through the microscope but then I become restless.

Perched on a lab stool one day, I feel the chill, the bondage of measuring tools, the silence without contours— and I imagine the endearing tantrum of poetry— a wild, profound, pure thing, shattering itself outside the lab for me; pacing, waiting for me. It is an agitation so powerful and empowering that I leave the flasks and the glass tubes to be broken by their own silence: an act of defiance that would be the first one in my writing life.

Tangles

Oversized photography equipment. Tangled wires.
In a corner, a dusky, crooked mirror.

Ami takes us to the studio for our first passport photos. I am
wearing a dress that reminds me of beets for its color and
glassy smooth texture. The passport is for a visit to India.

From her purse, Ami takes out cash, maybe forty-five rupees
for three passport photos and a formal portrait of all three
children together.

The rupee coin in India had had Empress Victoria engraved
on it for decades by the time my grandparents were born.
And around the time my parents were born, the earlier
struggle for independence from the British Empire was already becoming the struggle to settle the new nation of Pakistan— the crescent and star newly engraved on the currency.
By the year of my own birth, gone was that currency of my
parents' generation, those banknotes with the Bengali script;
only Urdu remained— East Pakistan had been split from
West Pakistan.

When India was partitioned from Pakistan, my young married aunts had stayed in India while my grandparents migrated with the rest of their children to Dhaka, East Pakistan. It was there my father had attended the American
school and prepared for college in the UK, my mother had
attended Dhaka University as an exchange student from Lahore, and it was there my parents were engaged.

When another partition was on the horizon, the one between
East and West Pakistan, the entire family moved to West Pakistan. In the late sixties, my father returned from London
and married my mother in Lahore.

I am negotiating wires and tripods, making my way to the mirror.

I have not yet met my family in India, just seen them in photos. The tension between India and Pakistan is apparent even to a child my age; I'm five. I know to love the India of my paternal grandmother, *Daadi jaan's* stories: mango orchards, trains to Calcutta, Persian expressions interwoven with Urdu, black silk evening *ghararas*. I'd imagine freshly made *Paan*, the sweet, leaf wrapped delicacy, every time I polished my grandmother's elaborate silver *paandaan* which was engraved with a verse in Persian and a phrase in Urdu on its small tray that said "janab e aali, paan hazir hai!" (a way of saying *Bon appetite!*), a trousseau item passed on to my mother, the eldest daughter-in-law of the family, and later to Bhai's wife Oksana, the eldest daughter-in-law of our generation.

Side by side with nostalgia inherited from family, is the sense that India is an aggressor, that we have a past made of war.

We would drive to Lahore, leave our blue Mazda at the Wahgah border, and catch a train across the Punjab border to India. In the stifling heat, my brothers and I entertain ourselves with our newly acquired *bansuri* or reed flute, making a racket, poking each other with it, and in less than an hour into the journey, we manage to annoy Ami so much that she tosses the flute out the window. When the train stops momentarily, a soft, lulling breeze blows across the stretch of green fields; we are quiet all of a sudden, aware that we have crossed the border into India. As the train slowly begins to move again, a man in a Sikh turban rushes to our window, out of breath, handing Ami the flute that he had seen flying out.

The retrieval of the flute will stay in my memory as a metaphor for the largeness of the human spirit, the flute being a symbol of the great Sufi tradition of Punjab, land of my birth and of this storied border with India.

My aunts' mannerisms and voices are immediately familiar, their energy, all love. Their kitchens are ecstatically busy, festive places, churning out the most delicious food: coconut samosas, sundried mango, pound cake, *biryani* and kababs. My memory of India will remain haloed by the feeling of being lovingly fed. I'll often wonder who I would have been if I had been part of the clan that never migrated.

As I make my way to the mirror now, I know who I am; both my brothers beside me, in the photo studio, my world is right here, and we are getting ready for new places.

Before the photo, our mother wants to do a final touch up; she rejects the lint-ridden hairbrush lying on a stool that the proprietor points to, quickly runs her fingers through our hair in lieu of a comb. Each of us face the camera, photographed for the first time for the purpose of identity.

Reading

Up until now, my brothers are my playmates, climbing trees and walls with me, getting into fights. Our final collaboration is a pond we dig in the yard
for our ducks.

There is also cricket with the neighbors' children, broken windowpanes, and the making of slingshots, setting paper on fire with a magnifying glass— at this point I lose interest. I know the boys will get into trouble sooner or later and I ease out of the club on the basis of not wanting to be reprimanded for digressions I don't particularly enjoy.

I want to take risks of my own, gratifying ones.

Having given up playing, I find myself deeply interested in painting. I paint with an obsessive zeal. I do crayons and pencils, then watercolors. The subjects that interest me most are found in books with pictures, such as Ami's text books from her evening Persian classes. Each of these books begins with what appears to be elaborate praise for the Shah of Iran, the first few pages devoted to full size portraits of each member of the royal family wearing fashionable Western outfits, the king's receding hairline, the women with their bouffant and frosted lips. It upsets me to find two queens and one king. I decide, only on the basis of pictures, that I like the older, sad-eyed Surayya better than the glamorous and insanely popular Farah Deeba. The illustrations that go with the text in these books are made in modern, bold strokes, unlike the tentative, smudgy illustrations in Urdu books. These books from the *Khana e Farhang e Iran* captivate me as much as the art in the house—the Renoir and Rembrandt prints my mother had bought on trips to Museums in New York and DC, the Pakistani artist Sadiquain's calligraphy, Japanese prints, and my favorite: oil on canvas, *The chapli kabab shop* by a local artist.

Much of what I'm taken by becomes enveloped in a small but distinct home of its own. At some point words replace my hunger for images and I turn to reading. When I begin writing, the books I read become recurring flashes of memory, each with its own universe of sensory experience: I'll remember sitting by the window, reading *Of Mice and Men* as the sky rages with all its monsoon might, the drama of rain in real life entering the world of the novel. I still see the pages in the other-worldly light of Peshawar rain.

And numerous other such moments: reading *Far from the Madding Crowd* on long summer afternoons, to the click-clicking of the ceiling fan, the faint aroma of lunch still in the air, lounging by the fire of the big gas heater at home in Peshawar, reading P.G. Wodehouse and eating hot *sohan halva* during winter-break. Or even farther back, my mother reading aloud from an old copy of "Mirat ul uroos," an Urdu classic— the light and shadows on its yellowed pages, her clear, soft voice, my eyes lingering on the corners of the white walls, watching my grandmother's glow-in-the-dark "time piece" from Mecca as I listened to the story.

A good book creates an uncanny silence, a bubble around the reader so that not only is the world of its offering lucid and deeply felt but the sensory reality of the moment is preserved: the smooth lamination on library books, the vanilla scent of the paper, the peculiar tone of light falling on the pages, the thumb, the forefinger, the luxurious corners of fabric-bound book, the dog-eared comfort of the folded paperback. Text blends in, binds with the texture of the sensory moment; the book becomes one with the reader.

The first digital book of poems I'll read, later in life, would be Fady Joudah's *Textu*. I'll approach the kindle with uncertainty, wondering how much the "reading device" will steal from me. As I'll fall into the rhythm of the short poems, their jagged, tender, stark, subtle world, I'd sense a hush, then a gradual letting in of the vivid sound of wind-chimes from the patio, the lamplight taking on the glow of Japanese paintings: a familiar filter of warmth from childhood.

These brief, dreamlike, lasting spells— the residue of the reading life— fills the writing life with the indispensable element: wonder. Once lodged in memory, it carries on— refilling, refueling.

Colors and Knots

In the winter, Peshawar reminds me of a slate; soberly, clinically gray except for some luscious butter-golden afternoons spent on the lawn. On such afternoons, we listen to music on our red cassette player. It is either Boney M. or ABBA.

We read and munch on dry fruit (peanuts, pine nuts, and "*kishmish*", or sultana raisins) that we keep in the pockets of our sweaters.

If friends of Ami's are visiting, there are bags on the grass next to them with balls of wool, the bright yarn snaking up to the clicking needles. My mother knits only when she is inspired, not out of seasonal habit. She knits rather well and mostly for me but her knitting will motivate me less to learn knitting myself, more to read everything like a weave: poetry, history, faces. Working with hands—be it sewing, painting, cooking—is of less value in this house than reading or having a solid conversation, typically over a meal or tea.

From conversations between adults, occasionally Abi's work associates—guests from abroad, or local friends, writers and artists who visit, I learn that the world is much bigger and more varied than I can imagine, and its story is a weave that is impossible to decipher, and that our purpose here is to untangle. I don't have the patience for it, just as yet, but years from now I'll marry someone who has the mental stamina to puzzle over the complex weave, and the patience and dexterity to untangle. He will balance my restlessness, teach me to trust my own fingers; he'll prove that brilliance is found on the ground as much as the sky.

My eyes keep returning to the off-white and lavender mirrorwork of the tea cozy—tiny mirrors sewn into fabric remind me that each of us in this lifelong conversation are the same and different.

Knitting makes a comforting rhythm as we drink tea. China and stainless steel chime over the fitful crows, and the crisp *azan*, the call to prayer in Arabic with a *pushto* inflection. A winter *wudu* ablution is challenging in the absence of hot water if the geyser isn't working. Prayer breaks up the idyll and takes each freshly washed elder, servant, guest, child into a more personal space for a few minutes— *wudu* often the longer part of prayer.

My prayer rug of choice looks nothing like a regular prayer rug. A crochet-edged green cloth that Ami sewed herself, it became even more special when it turned yellow after I left it on the roof on the day of the solar eclipse; I like to think my eclipse-ripened *jai namaz* is a witness to celestial drama, the ferocity of which we had been warned against, having been told that if you look directly at the sun at the moment it is in eclipse, you go blind forever: my lime prayer rug turned guava-pale.

My maternal grandmother, Nani jaan, teaches me how to pray *namaz*. In the sunlit verandah, where she reads, combs her hair, offers her *namaz* covering herself with a blue checkered shawl, I find the slow pages of Plato's *Republic* or Iqbal's collected poems. She has been a professor for years and years; when she visits, she spends most of her time reading unless she is picking mulberries with me or telling me stories from Shakespeare's plays— my favorites are the ones that revolve around three choices and outspoken women: *King Lear* and *The Merchant of Venice*. Other stories I enjoy also include unusual female characters, such as Jane Eyre, or the one about the Qazi of Jaunpur. She drinks tea, I eat oranges. The stories are like homes in the wilderness— familiar, welcoming, fortifying. All the bullies at school, all the demons diminish and melt away. The art of the story has a peculiar majesty— it nurtures vision, it unties the knots of history.

Okra, mint and chilies grow in the back, and marigolds and roses in the front yard; they're in my peripheral vision as I bike and study. The seeing is important. On her visits, Nani jaan teaches me Qura'an and Math. Before she began teaching me and before I owned a student desk with wheels, I didn't care much for Math. It's now a ritual: I roll my desk out of my room to the verandah, bring a stack of paper and ask my grandmother to give me Math problems I can solve. I do this after my daily bike ride in the yard. My grandmother reads the newspaper while I work on equations. Occasionally, she shares a news item of interest. Twice I've seen her tear up reading about the brutality of the Indian military in Kashmir. She is a Kashmiri. She folds her spectacles and closes her eyes when I ask her for a story; it's typically the one from the Quran about Moses in a floating basket, how he chose coals over gold, and the knotting of his tongue. There is too much brutality in the world and not enough words. The knotted tongue resonates with me.

At the time of my grandmother's passing, I'm ten years old, and stay in shock for long. My mother later describes what was to be their last drive together—how she wiped her mother's glasses as they passed the river Ravi and historical Lahore. Ravi means narrator, storyteller. I imagine my grandmother as being rapt in the view of Ravi and the twelve doorways of the Mughal *bara dari*. Years later, I'll remember this moment of seeing through her eyes, when, in her beloved Kashmir, pellet guns are used by the Indian Military against Kashmiri protestors, many of them women—mothers— the unspeakable brutality of "dead eyes" in the midst of the living beauty of Kashmir.

Comb Maker

Her blindness   electric
A Silkworm's
delicate   eyeteeth industry

Was she once a whalebone—
Marbled Baleen plates of an ancient comb
herself?

Was she a captive-weaver
with only her skeletal toes to separate
and untangle the threads

A florescent filter   a tender fork in the road
A pronged cactus   a flayed spider
Truth teller of history

*"Look! Look again! and chumars, bankers and tinkers, barbers
and bunnias, pilgrims – and potters – all the world going and coming.
It is to me as a river from which I am withdrawn like a log after a flood.
And truly the Grand Trunk Road is a wonderful spectacle. It runs
straight, bearing without crowding India's traffic for fifteen hundred
miles – such a river of life as nowhere else exists in the world."*

Rudyard Kipling

Rooftop to Rooftop

"I'm on a roadside perch," writes Ghalib in a letter, "lounging on a *takht*, enjoying the sunshine, writing this letter. The weather is cold...," he continues, as he does in most letters, with a ticklish observation or a humble admission ending on a philosophical note, a comment tinged with great sadness or a remark of wild irreverence fastened to a mystic moment. These are fragments recognized in Urdu as literary gems because they were penned by a genius, but to those of us hungry for the short-lived world that shaped classical Urdu, those distanced from that world in time and place, Ghalib's letters chronicle what is arguably the height of Urdu's efflorescence as well as its most critical transitions as an elite culture that found itself wedged between empires—the Mughal and the British, and eventually, many decades after Ghalib's death, between two countries— Pakistan and India.

I write this on a winter day in California. It is Mirza's two hundred and twenty first birth anniversary. There is a nip in the air and the sunlight is filtered through my carob tree; my notes, scribbled in *Nastaliq*, are dappled and illuminated by sudden flashes as the branches sway. Isn't Ghalib's Delhi a labyrinth of dappled alleys, a dream leaping from rooftop to rooftop, getting a stealthy taste of the saffron-cream dessert known to be prepared here under a full moon and left overnight to set in winter dew— a heady mix of in-the moment-sensations that vivify memory— rising with the city's nimble frangipani, its famed red sandstone and marble minarets, returning reliably like its homing pigeons?

Watching an Indian film that revolves around Mughlai cuisine, my husband remarks that it makes him nostalgic for a place he knows without ever having visited; the culture is in our bones, being Pakistanis whose grandparents migrated from India to Pakistan around the time of the partition. As a student in Lahore, I loved viewing the silhouettes of Mughal buildings at night and in the winter fog, the contours of the poet Iqbal's home and burial place in the shimmer of the street vendors' lanterns, deep in the walled city. On recent visits, I see mustard fields blooming in winter sunshine, my brother's orchards and fields luxuriating in the most delectable shades of green. Only a few miles away from his farm, lies the "No Man's Land"— not much bigger than a cricket pitch. Beyond that, lies India.

I have often stood by the gate of guards and flags at the Barki border, gazing at the distant rice paddies and colorful turbans of India, reflecting on what brings the two countries together, what keeps them apart. Cities on borders are my lot, it seems, having been born in Lahore, raised in Peshawar and lived in San Diego for most of my life. I wish I could glide and hover over rooftops, alighting at will, caring only for the wind current and never minding the boundaries between countries.

And here, now, a cup of chai beside me on an octagonal table that Ami brought me from Lahore, I'm chewing on pods of cardamom as I write, leaning on velvet bolster cushions— the kind that Mirza must have used, reclining on his "takht" which is a simple wooden bedstead commonly used as a day bed in the garden or verandah. I have, before me, a set of lyrical photos of Old Delhi— taken by the illustrious Indian poet Sudeep Sen. These doors belong to the heart of Delhi, Mirza Ghalib's neighborhood; these are aged thresholds that have seen many tearful departures and arrivals— eyes, old and young, have longed for a loved one's face, have dreamed of hearing once again a familiar footfall.

Ghalib saw Delhi suffer unspeakable calamities after the war of 1857— known as the "Mutiny" or the "War of Independence" depending on whether you're on the side of the British Raj or the people of the Indian subcontinent. As the city fell, Ghalib wrote about it in bitterness, bemoaning the sorrows of the ordinary city-dwellers more than the city's physical devastations or its lost imperial glory. He had already said goodbye to the Mughal culture that was fast becoming a relic, but forever the Urdu poet wedded to the elusive beloved, he preserves for himself and for us the transcendental promise of love, its power and pluck:

dil hī to hai siyāsat-e-darbāñ se Dar gayā
maiñ aur jā.ūñ dar se tire bin sadā kiye

Merely a timid heart, it was frightened of the politics of the doorkeeper
Would I ever leave your door without calling out for you?

Hidden in this verse is a message for future poets to not be intimidated by boundaries and doorkeepers, to dare to sing the walls down and chase dreams leaping rooftop to rooftop.

Tor Khum, the Black Curve

Tor Khum, the border between Pakistan and Afghanistan, feels like an utter release— as if we are random things, a fistful of summer insects set free in space. This, of course, is before the Soviet War, when I am in elementary school. Dwarfed by the standoffish ice blue mountains on the road to Torkham, we love the bridge one must drive under twice, once before and once after a loop. Where Peshawar is a nest of "*jhoola* parks" with stone slides, school routine, snack bars, badminton at home for girls, street cricket for boys, Torkham is a rush of freedom.

Sunlight hits the rocks here in a way that keeps shadows minimal, the boundlessness is the essence of the place and a contradiction to the bitterly disputed Durand line, the artificial boundary that stares you in the eye with a chilling animosity. This corridor between countries, this no-man's land, is sobering, even though at my age I know nothing of the long and bloody history of empire, of the great game of the not so distant past, and I certainly have no clue that we stand on the terra firma where an imminent series of wars will impact global history.

My brothers enjoy the treeless, rugged mountains, the wide embrace of the sun, the cool wind whipping, *shalwars* swelling like sails. I prefer to gaze at this generosity of grayness, angularity and sun from the café window. There is only one café, with nothing on the menu except for Coca-Cola and tea sandwiches but the place is magical and never feels lacking in anything. Peshawar being desperately short of tourist attractions, my father brings his overseas guests to Tor Khum. We come here so often that Nomi, only four years old at the time, serves as a perfect tourist guide, somehow communicating to the Japanese, British, or American guests all the tourist worthy aspects of a place more historical than any of us realize then.

Driving along the Khyber Pass I know vaguely that this is the ancient route of famous invaders. Alexander the Great had come through here; descendants of his army, light-eyed, dark-haired pagans still populate the Northern areas—*Kafiristan*, a fringe culture of slave-musicians, wine, trading of women and other such customs still ensconced in a country with a Muslim majority now. Hindus, Zoroastrians, Muslims, Sikhs, and Christians have all had dramatic battles around these parts through the centuries. The rocks have absorbed war cries in many tongues and all I remember is their amnesiac aloofness and silence.

As an adult, I would recall these mountains when I read passages from the *Baburnama* (memoirs of the founder of the Mughal dynasty) to my children. It fascinates me how the Mongols, who had decimated Muslim cultures, setting libraries on fire in Baghdad and Persia in one generation, themselves became Muslims in the next and became patrons of the arts as Mughals. And how Babur in his memoir reminisces about his lush and lovely Ferghana with fountains and Persian-style gardens; the more he travelled east into India the more he missed the natural and cultivated beauty of his homeland. *There are no beautiful buildings, gardens or beautiful women in India,* he proclaimed. His dynasty was to last for over three hundred years and to make India synonymous with breathtaking architecture and gardens.

The arrangement of space has an effect on the psyche. I love Peshawar for *Masood Toy Shop* and *Saeed Book Bank*, for lunch and swimming at the club; I am less at ease with its hypocrisies, overt racism— life outside of the oasis of my parents' relatively more urbane sensibilities. My parents, both emigrés, despite their genuine, growing attachment to the city, negotiate a tough balance between assimilation and forging their own path, becoming part of a progressive tide: a very important life lesson and one I will recall often when I move to the US after marriage.

My parents' struggle to adapt in an otherwise parochial society is especially apparent in their efforts to raise a daughter with the same privileges as their sons. It takes some fighting to compensate for a lopsided culture; on the occasion of my birth, my father goes against tradition and offers four sacrificial lambs (to each of my brothers' two), weighs my baby-hair against gold to give alms in gratitude, as is the custom, and my paternal grandmother, Daadi jan, herself the mother of six lovingly raised daughters, orders copious amounts of sweetmeats to be distributed in celebration—unusual in a society where the birth of a girl is not so much an occasion of joy as reticence. Daughters, on both side of my family, are cared for as much as sons. My family, including grandparents, tend to make a statement of equality when they can but they avoid direct confrontation; Ami and Abi, and their respective families tend to draw a line between moral courage and out and out rebellion.

My parents try to make up for the lack of opportunities without making a fuss. They send me to the same school as my brothers, the only co-ed school in the city, and in the absence of easily accessible opportunities for sports outside of school, they drive me long distances for squash and swimming lessons in an all-female club.

Life for an ambitious girl in Peshawar is no less than a hurdle race, isolating, and at times overwhelming. The only place where I'll really let my hair down is home.

The mountains of Tor Khum, or "black curve," on the other hand, will be conjured in my mind every time I feel heady with independence as a young adult living in Pakistan and abroad. The fiercely sculpted mountains are a persona representing the empowering surge of freedom. Soon I would witness the ravages of war in these parts, the Afghans fighting against the Soviets; decades later, the new century would bring a new war and the word "freedom" in American-English would ironically become a euphemism for imperial expansion and ideological control. Where in my teenage years I became used to television images of Americans celebrating the "Mujahideen," those engaged in "Jihad," in my adulthood, "Jihad" would become a dirty word, and allies would become enemies.

After decades of violence in the area, I dare not imagine the café or the scenes visible through the window I loved. Tor Khum, I am sure, is still flint-mouthed, large and self-possessed, still defiant against every brand of empire.

Persimmon Veil, Piercing Eyes

Like others of my generation, my first exposure to violence is through images shown in the evening news on TV. We grow accustomed, as children in the '70s and '80s, to seeing tanks, machine guns, explosions, distressed faces—most often of people from Muslim cultures— Kashmir, Palestine, Iran, Iraq, Bosnia, Somalia, and others. Of all wars and conflicts, the one most immediate and traumatic is the one across the border from my hometown, in Afghanistan.

From the faces and voices of the refugees I know that they come from a culture very similar to the culture of *Sarhad* (the "Frontier") or Khyber Pukhtunkhua, the province where Peshawar is located. One of my first memories of being in awe is the memory of watching the cityscape change over-night; Jamrud, the Western end of the Grand Trunk Road, the historic highway which seemed expansive and tranquil, even godforsaken on some of the stretches, is now filled with crowds of people, mostly very tall, turbaned men, but also by burka-clad women and small children. As a seven-year old, my attention is absorbed by the youngest of the refugees; this is the first time I have seen children with missing limbs. I'm overcome by sadness and horror when I hear about the Soviets luring children by placing toys in landmines:

> I remember how a crippled child
peeled a tangerine one December morning,
and how the citrus dew made a strange mist
in the sun, and how it took only a moment
for this sweet, wet dust to disappear
the way the shiny toy had disappeared
when he had reached for it,
back when he was in Kabul.
That is how the Russians had burnt
a little boy's limbs.
> I remember his eyes: Indus-blue and lost.

Indus, the river of invaders and exiles, blue, as is the color the mountains take on now with the refugees crossing. In my book *Kohl and Chalk*, I'll remember the overwhelming toll of war and the irony of borders— recalling an instance before the war when my friend and I, both aged six, were reprimanded by Afghan guards simply for straddling the rope that marked the border in the barren mountains of Tor Khum, a symbol of sovereignty and separation in the vast rocky wilderness, deserving more respect than the act of our planting a foot each and yelling "look, we're in two countries at once!" showed.

Months later, Afghan families flood across this same border. And by joining the Afghan/USA side of the war against the Soviet Union, we do find ourselves in two countries at once.

Stepping Across the Border

From my home window
    Prussian blue
Mazda's window
    broken glass blue
my school's window
    carbon-paper blue

Mountains
    circled my life like a spell
in blue

At *Tor Khum*
    they were touching distance
Was it charcoal or chalk or rope
    that marked the border?
Afghanistan was just beyond a slim crease of blue

Before being warned by the guards
   I had moved my foot across
To step into what would later become ash blue

The guards made me step back
   gave me a water-melon
I was only a child under the spell of mountains
   Out of which I would later see
refugees flow
   River blue   Bruise blue

In the refugee camp not far from where I live, a photographer takes an iconic photo of a girl wearing a torn persimmon-colored veil. She has piercing green eyes and an unforgettable gaze. The photo, published in the *National Geographic* magazine, becomes an internationally acclaimed image known by the name "The Afghan Girl" and brings fame to the photographer Steve McCurry.

The subject of this famous photograph is, for a long time, a girl without a name. Decades later, when Steve McCurry realizes that he knows nothing about the subject whose photograph earned him a name, he will return to her refugee camp in Peshawar in search of her. He will track her down with difficulty since too much will have changed to effectively search for a nameless refugee with only a childhood similitude to go by. He will have numerous failed attempts going through green eyes belonging to women of roughly the same age. Finally, with the help of scanning technology, he will find grownup Sharbat Gula, take new photographs of her and publish these new photographs along with her life story. When I read the published details, I discover that Sharbat Gula, the girl with the piercing eyes, is not only nearly the same age as myself, she belongs to a refugee camp located only a few miles away from where I grew up.

Sharbat Gula's story will bring back that time, and I will write a ghazal in response many years later. When published in my book *Ghazal Cosmopolitan*, I'll revisit the story repeatedly as I pick the poem for reading events in the US and abroad, most memorably to audiences of young people—students in Pakistan, Kyrgyzstan and Turkey, where the next generation of Afghans have lived since birth, and to whom the Afghan girl is a legend from another era.

Ghazal for the Girl in the Photo

You became the girl with the piercing eyes when you found
your country swiped by a stranger
In Kabul snow, a missile turned your mother into coal, your
last tears were wiped by a stranger

A garden once hung from your name like the perfume of
wild apple blossoms, phantom tulips
In the refugee camp, are you Sharbat Gula, *liquor of flowers*,
or a number typed by a stranger?

Your eyes teach how cold flint ignites a flare, how a father's
bones become an orphan's roof
History writes itself clear as cornea, your green glare—no
whitewashing, no hype is stranger

Pity the empire that failed to decipher the disdain in your
eyes, the hard stare of war
Pity the first world's pity, the promise of friends who show
up as every type of stranger

Zeest, return to the arms of memory, the riddle of its
minefields, velvet lullabies
To the lilt of this land, its lyrical storms, its bells and
bagpipes, you're no stranger

Equal as the Teeth of a Comb

Ami does my hair in Helen of Troy style, a high pony tail with strands wrapped around it on days there is extra time before school. She remembers the hairdo from an old movie which she talks about often, along with her other favorite *The Taming of the Shrew* with Liz Taylor. When she combs, she hums, mostly Urdu songs, occasionally Punjabi. Since settling in Peshawar, she has taught herself Pashto not only because it isn't easy to run a household and her myriad projects without knowing the local language, but because she has a genuine love for connecting with people of all kinds, everywhere. We joke that she can make friends while crossing the road; this is something she and I don't have in common. I tend to be withdrawn, like my father, content with my books and thoughts.

There are times when I do enjoy going on outings, especially when Ami takes me on an excursion to the old city and shows me how herbs, spices, henna, tealeaves, and grains of every kind are sold box-less, displayed in smooth mounds. I like to walk through the narrow streets with her, taking in the crisp, salty aroma of street food, the colors of sherbets, glass bangles, sparkly trim for *dupattas*, watching shopkeepers with their paraphernalia— their weighing scales, aluminum scoops and glossy brown paper bags. The joy of walking through a bazar, which will become a subject I'll explore for years in my writing, begins here. I feel certain that if I were to put my ear to the ground, I'll hear the tread of Silk Road caravans. My curiosity about how cultures of encounter are formed and revealed in the marketplace— about trade- and work habits, competition and conflict, creative marketing, the ethos of fairplay and equality and the complex dynamics of cosmopolitanism— is born as a result of watching my mother interact. I'm astonished by how she varies the language or dialect, accent or register, "code-switching" naturally as she goes.

Peshawar's cosmopolitanism pulsates behind its ancient walls. This legendary thoroughfare, valley of flowers praised by emperors, and of teashops where traders brought many worlds together, where the imperial collided with the mercantile and spiritual through the millennia, is obscured by its shadow self: a city stubbornly resistant to newcomers and to change, addicted to custom. I find its immutable tribalism unsettling for many reasons, but most importantly because the idea of equality is ingrained in me as a basic Islamic value. I'm taught at a young age to have a filter against discrimination, whether in stories or history, real life situations, TV dramas or politics. It is the principle at the heart of my belief system. I listen intently for balance. I ask if Helen of Troy had a say in the matter of launching "a thousand ships and burning the topless towers of Ilium." I commit to memory Shylock's powerful soliloquy:

"Hath not a Jew eyes? hath not a Jew hands, organs,
dimensions, senses, affections, passions? fed with
the same food, hurt with the same weapons, subject
to the same diseases, healed by the same means,
warmed and cooled by the same winter and summer, as
a Christian is?" (The Merchant of Venice Act 3, Scene 1)

I ask why, around us, the dark-skinned Christians were subjected to slurs, called "sweepers" while the light-skinned were held in awe and called "*Sahibs*," why non-Pashto speakers were considered inferior, and women were stigmatized for a host of reasons that men were not, such as being childless, unmarried or divorced, why we judge different human beings by different standards.

The Prophet of Islam, himself from a tribal society, rejected tribalism and discrimination. From watching *The Message* as a child, I remember the moment when the elite tribesmen of

Quresh are stunned at the idea that Islam considers all people to be equal— "as equal as the teeth of a comb"— and that there is no claim of merit of an Arab over a non-Arab, or of white over a black person, or of a male over a female, only God-fearing people merit a preference with God. Equal as the teeth of a comb. Now, and throughout my life, I'll continue to see gross violations of the principle of equality among the people who claim to be the Prophet's followers and this phrase will often return to me.

At this age I tag along with Ami in her red Toyota Corolla, never fully admitting that I'm fascinated by how she selects everything from fabric to fruit, how she can make herself comfortable in all social situations, maintaining the same level of respect and consideration even as I hear her code-switching while speaking to a yogurt seller, a washerwoman, an electrician, a hairdresser, the school principal, the dentist, or the Governor. She manages with courteousness and a sense of humor, while remaining authentic and getting things done. I, on the other hand, find our class-ridden society too distressing; I don't confront it though I care deeply and wish for change. While she turns and churns her many languages, I'll funnel all of mine in the language of poetry, shutting out the speakers, keeping their concerns close.

Despite my insular lifestyle, I know that the residents of this great city are warm-hearted and true of purpose, and I also know that their tribalism limits their potential and draws strange boundaries of alienation and attachment in relation to the place I call home. I identify and resist its narrow confines and selective loyalties— reminiscent of that most unfortunate combination of arrogance and ignorance characterized as "*jahaliya*" by scholar Karen Armstrong. The mystics and thinkers I read all lead me away from tribal attitudes, towards cosmopolitanism. Years later, when I go to Lahore to study at Kinnaird, I'll tell my father that I miss home but I couldn't be happier to have the opportunity to experience life in an intellectually open and stimulating environment, where voices different from one another have a better chance at being valued equally, where balance is possible.

As a student in Lahore, I feel terribly nostalgic when the sky turns a certain hue, or I catch a whiff of guavas or the delicate golden *sundarkhani* grapes or I overhear the sound of Pashto—I miss the sights, scents and sounds of home and the company of family friends, local as well as transplants, whom I'll continue to miss later when I move to America, when the houses of childhood playmates appear in recurring dreams. One of the voices of Peshawar that infuses my memories with the deepest joy is the voice of Ami's friend, the Pashto poet and professor Zeenat Khattak, who is among the most vivacious, spiritual, and loving people I've known. Her example teaches me that a poet's subtlety of feeling and refinement of thought are possible to cultivate even where a gruff absolutism reigns supreme. I'm friends with her daughters throughout my young days but as I grow older I find a special kindred spirit in her— the only female poet with whom I have Peshawar in common, the only one who gives the city's memory a many-faceted, mystic glimmer. Her sideways profile, with a rose in her hair, is forever part of the mythos I build of Peshawar.

Notes for a Combing Song

Shall we begin with a comb and an empty field
(jeweled grass, November sun, long-necked
bottle of mustard oil)?

I'll never believe there is time enough
to untangle from (-tango with) our shadow selves

but let's try all the same. Bring a radio,
a week's worth of *The Frontier Post*

for drips, bring a thermos of chai, a clear
mind, some kind of winter halva with blanched almonds,

a *Namda* rug— itchy, but as you know, its gigantic
tawny-maroon daisies and juicy green ferns

are reminders that the universe
has a big heart. It is tightlipped but true.

Maybe you'll align shadow
with shadow, cover my new periwinkle

sweater with a towel before oiling
and braiding my hair.

Maybe you'll let the cats yowl in the distance, the cauliflower
overcook, fill the dialer with marbles, let the phone ring.

Train Tracks

If there is a thought urgent enough to return to, it comes on a train and is cut off at my station. All the rest is an obsessive plan to go back, find the nodes and connect them.

At 23, I'll move to San Diego with my husband. Having grown up in a valley, I'll be petrified to live so close to the ocean— with its flat expanse, blind depths, and a refrain that seems to say *go home, go home.* But then I'll discover tree-lined train tracks along the coast and know I belong.

Train tracks, long walks, trees; the journey, the hopping on and off. My first home in Peshawar is close to train tracks; tranquil, rich with ghosts and trees.

The Eucalyptus trees with their peeling bark, flesh and russet, their presence like the sculptures in Paris gardens, deceptively human and vulnerable. They tower above— slender and superior. I admire their poise but identify better with the oak: tree of intertwined stories, *Alif Laila* tales, tangle of endlessly connecting plots that grow out of each other, a wild cluster— the clumsy, protean shape, perhaps, of the soul.

The train tracks are serene and peopled by invisible journeymen; spirits of the past filling the sharp Eucalyptus-scented air with the energy of endless passage. Didn't Kipling travel to Peshawar on *dak-rail* as a special correspondent for the *Civil and Military Gazette*, and Jinnah, Pakistan's founding father, step out of a train to cheering crowds when he delivered his famous speech at Islamia College? These are the trees, and this, the crystalline valley surrounded by the *Safed Koh* mountains they must have seen.

Kipling invented several characters (in fiction and poetry) belonging to Peshawar. In his *Ballad of East and West*, his character Kamal says to his son:

So thou must eat the White Queen's meat, and all her foes are thine,
And thou must harry thy father's hold for the peace of the border-line.
And thou must make a trooper tough and hack thy way to power—
Belike they will raise thee to Ressaldar when I am hanged in Peshawur.

Ghosts of history and fiction reside in train booths; suppressed questions hanging in corners; scenes from another time and place I feel I have witnessed: Raj trains where the natives were kept separate from the ruling British, India/Pakistan Partition trains bringing the massacred, cut up dead; such tragedies, but also reunions, wedding parties, great epiphanies, thought experiments of relative motion, songs and stories that sustain.

On my earliest walk on the street that runs parallel to the tracks, I remember a child-sized umbrella and a box (with a picture of a chubby hen) that opens to show as if from a window the multicolored egg-shaped candies inside: these are things to buy from *Town Store*, a place of infinite excitement before we are old enough to know *Masood Toys*, and later Karachi's *Fun Land*, or California's *Disneyland*.

The last time I walk along those train tracks, I have a vague sense that things are changing fast and we may not come here ever again for leisurely walks. Bhai is already at boarding school, I am a perpetually worried middle-schooler; Nomi, more pragmatic than I, has less trouble adapting. Far ahead in practical wisdom, he has taught me everything from lighting a match at age five, reaching the counter by climbing a chair and operating the toaster, to interesting vernacular and selling and buying a car when we're adults.

At this time, Peshawar is brimming with Afghan refugees and Western Aid workers; it will be dubbed "the spy capital of the world." We can no longer remember what life was like before the Soviet War.

Walking home, on a quiet December night, I wish for time to slow down. How much longer will the salted corn with the aroma of charcoal and hot sand be made and sold in small paper bags made out of pages from old notebooks? Will it be years or months until we stop listening to Radio Moscow on our drive to school, and Abi to BBC every night? Not long at all.

In future years I would take trains on three different continents, lose and find thoughts, but this would be the last winter I would wear my mother's hand-knitted sweaters.

That last walk along train tracks in Peshawar ends in halogen street lighting: a dream's flash.

Chaðar of the Heart

One autumn I'm suddenly taller than my mother. The ecstasy of wearing her heels and blouses will, for an instant, distract me from the loss of inhabiting the innocence of a child's body—the hundred scents and stains of tumbling on grass, the anthills and hot powdery breath of brick-walls climbed, the textures of twigs and branches and wet doll hair and rubber bands, kite paper and tamarind-candy wrappers, the cicada-like sound of pencil sharpeners, the popping of coca cola bottle caps, of cracking pine nuts in the long winter evenings—will blunt and vanish, one by one.

That the sensory life is dulled just as the cerebral life is intensified, is no accident; at school, boys and girls are separated for a special talk on how the changing body requires a set of rules, a sense of restraint. The talk is grave and ends with alarming details of the impending burden of academic work that will make or break us. As if the process of adapting to a new life in a new body were not hard enough, we are told that we are under scrutiny for following the prescribed path of success as well as for containing the challenges that gender poses.

The body is as unforgiving as the social norms it finds itself in the clutches of; it is more often a tempest than a temple. Growing pains, at least for girls, must be strictly private. How you decipher and piece together the physical, emotional and social puzzle of your life is entirely and urgently your own responsibility and never without open and free scrutiny and judgement. The present is a perpetual shore to an ocean of future anxiety; there is no turning back. Without sisters or close female company, I am alone now in this space of being a girl and I always will be as a woman.

I wish to throw a tantrum. It is highly inappropriate for a girl to throw a tantrum, so I want, at age fourteen, to cry in the voice of a seven-year old boy: a good student, a mini law-abiding citizen, who bawls with conviction, his sobs not inwardly tuned but coming with a perfect pitch and tempo, blasting like the sharp maneuvers of a well-formed argument or a fast car. His school uniform is immaculate, hair is neatly cut, not a wisp straying; his demeanor demands respect. He may cry with abandon; there is no impure suggestion, no question to cover this youthful beauty or vulnerability from a stranger's gaze, no question of a veil; he is already beyond objectification, not yet a man. Being male, his grief is gold, not a sign of weakness but a bearing down of true burden. Tears fall on his leg, one perfectly polished shoe across his mother's lap. His mother is an invisible cup, allowing his tears to fall with the unbridled energy of having been wronged and being totally in the right. There is no controversy, self-pity, no breathless justification. The crying itself is a perfectly natural and noble response. She holds her sunglasses in one hand and in the other, holds his hand. Hers is a wordless, reverent devotion, as if she is in the presence of the Dalai Lama or Pope. Little hero flails in slow motion now, hair blowing madly in the wind.

When the wind nudges the door ajar, I see a wolf locking eyes with me. It's already too late. There is no room for negotiation in this red gaze. My time is up. The next scene will show a deep stain of annihilation on the kitchen floor. Besides this, I see in great detail, car accidents. Here, time slows down to the extent that I wish my time were up; glass shards in lungs, highway sounds exponentially louder, like the inside of a bell tower. Other moments, I find myself hiding, retching in the smoke-filled, putrid streets of bombed cities, afraid to cough or exhale, hearing clearly the footfall of military boots.

Fear, as much as grief, is to be kept tucked in, hidden from view.

I learn early to withhold tears in public. Crying attracts voyeurs or spectators who have pity, not sympathy. It lets off a spark of the soul's deepest sorrow before the eyes of those who will lust after a defeated girl, their eyes aglow with victory, the door ajar. If I were a seven-year old dignified boy, no one would doubt the power of my grief; crying would be an act of protest, not weakness.

Home seems more and more a strange island in Peshawar; a protective space where Bhai has taught me to ride a bike, given me boxing lessons and put up colorful lights in the verandah for our impromptu stage shows and Nomi makes me laugh and shows me recorded episodes of *Perfect Strangers*. We do not observe *purdah* as is customary in Peshawar society. My mother dresses fairly modestly in public but does not cover with a *chadar*— not an act of rebellion, just confidence in her philosophy that there is no need to follow modesty as dictated by the prescribers of the white *chadar*. She walks fearlessly past gawking men when we go shopping in Kuchi bazaar or Saddar, the crowded parts of town. Her timbre remains soft and feminine whereas I am far less comfortable and develop a veneer for my true voice with a curt, authoritative tone to ward off male attention. I make my gait purposeful, my expression guarded.

As teenagers we are expected to socialize with whoever comes to our house. Some of these occasions are ideal situations for hiding in the bathroom. When you are locked in there with soaps, towels, a mirror and a window with a view of trees, you feel soothed; it is rare to be forced out. I continue to find shelter in a secluded restroom even as a grown up. When I go to Vermont in 2000, the prestigious Bread Loaf Writers conference, I am away from my babies for the first time— Yaseen is two and Yousuf, five-months old. They are with my husband and mother, under excellent care, but I feel distressed, likely because I am a nursing mother and separation is almost traumatic. Between readings and workshops I must express milk in plastic bottles, dump them, fill them again, or the supply won't last the ten days of the conference and will stall my ability to nurse; the baby's vulnerability is my vulnerability, the body proves, once again, to be both powerful and vulnerable. Wandering the Bread Loaf campus, I find the most scenic and private bathroom, deep in the library, overlooking the tennis courts. Here, I cry my heart out.

It may be in the nature of demons to never go away, only grow as we grow, keeping up with our expanding faculties. They are, after all, masks of reality, its constants, the core of recurring nightmares. We brave more than we can bear to list. I find solace, as a young, sister-less girl, in stories of girls, my favorite being Louisa Alcott's *Little Women*. Abi brings me the whole series, the set of four books, from a trip to London. The character I identify with the most is the passionate, strong-willed, even a bit clumsy and cranky Jo, who is an aspiring writer. Deeply sensitive to her family's vulnerabilities, Jo puts up a rough, protective exterior. The most unforgettable moment of the story is when she sells her hair to a wig-maker to enable her mother to cover travel expenses as she takes a train journey to look after her injured father:

"My dear, where did you get it? Twenty-five dollars! Jo, I hope you haven't done anything rash?"

"No, it's mine honestly. I didn't beg, borrow, or steal it. I earned it, and I don't think you'll blame me, for I only sold what was my own."

As she spoke, Jo took off her bonnet, and a general outcry arose, for all her abundant hair was cut short.

"Your hair! Your beautiful hair!" "Oh, Jo, how could you? Your one beauty." "My dear girl, there was no need of this." "She doesn't look like my Jo any more, but I love her dearly for it!" (15.41-44)

Later that night, overcome by sadness and a sense of loss, the fierce, loving and resourceful Jo sobs and sobs into her pillow.

Outside the City

Says the Chinese
Pilgrim
HiuenTsang

There is   a Pipala tree
about
a 100 feet or so   in   height
Its branches   are   thick   (he notes   in 629 CE)

And the shade

Beneath

Somber

and

Deep

The past 4
Buddhas have sat

Beneath

this tree

and at the present
time
there are 4
sitting figures
of the Buddhas
to be seen here

Combing in Groves of the Jinn

Jinn: a spirit capable of appearing in human and animal forms and influencing humankind for either good or evil.

I recall long hair, coconut oil, the slow combing and the washing with scented *amla*, the advice to keep away from the sprawling Oak and Tamarind which may be inhabited by the jinn—not my personal memory, rather a sense passed down.

A startling laugh, low as if muffled by a *dupatta*, an old net *dupatta* I imagine, makes me turn but there is no one there. The walls are the color of vanilla ice cream and the décor is simple and modern apart from a few objects like doilies with Baluchi embroidery, an heirloom *paandaan*, a tray from the copper bazaar. This is Bhai's home in Lahore; there are the usual consumer electronics and curtains in a thick, embossed fabric— good for darkening the room against the defeating heat. A whiff of *chambeli* oil hangs in the punishing late June air for a moment. I recall how the jinn are attracted to fragrances too sweet on the human olfactory scale. Like animals, the jinn have a different wavelength for sensory perception. That low laugh might have actually been much lower or higher for non-human ears, the scent not as sickly sweet. Both probably came from the realm of the jinn, though my rational mind would not allow that thought.

Rumor has it that the maid, a middle aged stocky woman, is either a jinni in human form or a medium for the jinn. She speaks only when spoken to but she speaks in two distinct timbres: one, an ordinary female voice, the other heavy like gravel, a wolf-like growl. It's hard to predict how the next utterance will sound, whether it will come from the woman or the jinn she houses in her body. Her name is Ishrat, which means luxury. In Urdu Ishrat is a male name too. She is barely noticeable in my peripheral vision in her hand-me-down lawn outfit in candy colors as she goes about her usual cooking and cleaning but then her eyes meet mine in the mirror she is dusting. I feel a chill when I glimpse her classic jinn face—eyebrows arching high over the most ancient eyes— eyes brimming with the intense heat of summer afternoons, quicksand eyes that one will descend into uncontrollably; nose—an alignment of broken things, forehead vertiginously high like the ceiling of old train stations.

I don't want the jinn to detect my loss of composure. I reach for the tea tray she has placed next to my stack of books. The sound of china is comforting and when I go back to my reading, I tell myself never to look into those eyes again. Extracting myself won't be easy the next time. I'm pulled by the weight of the long afternoon, its lull, and Urdu's sonorous script, each looping "laam" and "noon" cradling me, but I cannot let myself fall asleep in Ishrat's presence.

The minute I close my eyes, I'm reminded of other jinns I've known in stories. There was one that possessed my aunt when she was six or seven— a docile and petit girl, she acquired superhuman strength for no apparent reason and became capable of knocking down several grown men at a time until she was exorcized. This was the India of my imagination and my grandmother's memories where women who were careless about covering their hair when they were near aged trees were certain to attract the attention of the jinn.

There were multi-story houses in these memories—monkeys climbing onto balconies and stealing food from the pantry or precious jewelry from the bedside tables of napping girls. Such stories belonged in different houses that the family lived in and different periods of their lives but for me they all take place in the house my imagination assembled—jinns on the upper floor, mangoes from the orchard ripening in the basement, my father and his cousin donning the Fez to please their grandfather in the courtyard, a young aunt, the shyest one, finding a snake and killing it with a shoe, in the kitchen. And always an open window, always a way for an old tree to be let in; a murmur, a songbird, a sparkling voice cutting through those dust-laden times.

I've never lived in a house with a courtyard or basement but even in a house with the requisite modern "global" influences represented by Japanese drawings, Renoir and Picasso prints, Islamic calligraphy calendars, the jinns were never too hard to imagine. A yellowed page from a book, a cat prowling at night, a sudden shadow leaping over a wall seen from the corner of my eye, and especially on long summer afternoons when street dogs pant and crows agitate the stillness, when there is a sweet whiff of rose syrup sherbet—I have no doubt I'm not alone.

Monsoon

Heat is eerie: lipsticks left unrefrigerated melt into deformity, ice cream liquefies and renders the scoop useless; fruit- and flower stalls carry the smell of that peculiar cusp between ripe and rotten.

Then rain comes, licking the sky green; the veil between the mysteries and the sun-weary, bleached, and hardened world dissolves away, becoming thin as a glassy insect wing. A dusty estrangement washes out, newly woven silken webs everywhere; meditation is possible again.

Clarity makes me humble: I'm smaller than a melon seed, slighter than a fishbone. I'm the moisture in the air and the movement in antennae; I'm filament and feelers, the quiver within the quiver, the wet crease in the smallest leaves. I'm also a rusty door hinge, static on television, soaked clothesline, scurrying lizard, the moving minute hand on the timepiece that is suddenly ticking louder; Rain changes the acoustics entirely— each syllable, sob, twitter, footfall, turning of a knob, is distinct. The airwaves have cleared and the cosmic channels open up.

I watch the raindrops make rings on the surface of a mossy cistern: water bangles! I imagine the continuously disappearing rain bangles on my wrists. Leaves float, throats are stirred into singing: a frog's croaking has a timbre of energy today, as if it is charging the earth in its deep, steady way.

Birdsong becomes an articulation in a foreign tongue I long to translate and memorize. I'm filled with a peaceful attentiveness. I listen like just another creature, to the sound of rain and the rustling and chirping in response. It occurs to me that the overpowering heat of summer hurts every sparrow, toad and tree as much as it hurts us. It also occurs to me that the heat has a maddening effect—we build rage, boil over, our spirits wilt, our vision blurs as if in sweat, our demons hover incessantly; we lose focus of the essence. It is a defeat of the soul because the body is under an immense attack.

Over the years, there have been many droughts and deaths due to water shortage in Pakistan. Those who did not die or suffer bodily harm have certainly felt the influence of the hot climate on their psyche. I recall connecting road accidents, brawls, conflicts, lethargy, and depression to the infernal heat.

The Sultans and Mughals made gardens and designed cross-ventilated buildings to stay cool in this land. The West made air conditioners. Pakistan has been in limbo— advanced enough to acquire energy-consuming, heat-producing vehicles and appliances, not advanced enough to have an uninterrupted energy supply to support them. The result is a nightmare: a constantly weakening relationship with nature and fellow humans. Vegetation is replaced with complexes upon complexes of flats and business plazas—buildings that are not in harmony with the climate. "Load shedding" or scheduled power outages have, for decades, decreased productivity and debilitated the system. The rich have their air conditioned cars and houses, and some have generators for use during power outage hours; the poor suffer incessantly, putting all their energies into survival and inevitably failing to improve the quality of life in the long run.

There is an inexplicable desolation in the sun's blinding glare, the parched vegetation, panting animals, fast rotting food, amplified chaos in the city. It can be compared to solitary confinement: the heat seems to burn the thread that joins us to the world around us. This desolation of being severed from everything, even ourselves, is expressed in the lexicon: "Cloud" and "rain" have welcome connotations, as if they will relieve us from alienation and bring the relief of reuniting. "Abr e karam" is "cloud of mercy," "baran e rehmat" is "rain of mercy;" "badal" (cloud) is a metaphor for shade and sanctuary. As children we would chant in unison "barrish baarish" (rain) standing by the windows, thrilled by the downpour. Later, I discovered that the desire for rain ran deep in the culture's roots. A great classical tune *Raag malhaar*, and hundreds of folk- and classical songs have been written and sung in praise of rain.

A drizzle releases a subtle musk that makes one fall head over heels in love with the soil. Heavy rain often follows, with gusts of wind moving in wide arcs. Thresholds and stairs collect pools of new rain, curtains get drenched. It's a wild embrace. From verandahs and windows we watch the spectacle: the ghostly shroud of dust, the thorny, forbidding feeling is gone. We are cleansed and alive. Children go to the rooftops to bathe in the rain, mothers cook special treats— "pakoray" (gram flour fritters), samosas, and hot syrupy "jalebi" with chai. As with everything else, celebration accompanies food, chatter, and song. I like time to myself, sitting by a window, reading by lamplight, feeling wildly alive but secretive and snug like Thumbelina in her walnut shell.

Rope of Hair

"Rapunzel, Rapunzel, let down your hair, so that I may climb the golden stair:" the witch sings to the blonde Repunzel imprisoned in her tower.

In a legend, Rudabeh, the dark-haired princess of Kabul lets her hair down like a rope for prince Zal to climb up to her tower. She has eyes "like the narcissus and lashes that draw their blackness from the raven's wing." Her name, Rudabeh, means "child of the river."

Repunzel is Brothers Grimms' nineteenth century retelling of *Persinette* (1689), which is surmised to be an adaptation of the millennia old Persian legend of Rudabeh recast in *Shanameh*, the Persian masterpiece written by the poet Firdowsi in the eleventh century. Firdowsi's lofty praise in his poem set a high bar for the artists who painted the legendary beauty of Rudabeh: "about her silvern shoulders two musky black tresses curl, encircling them with their ends as though they were links in a chain."

As a child, the links between stories from the East and the West emerge first through startling common etymologies in everyday language, songs and stories, then through reading about the history of the Silk Road. I read fairy tales in English from the left to the right side and stories of the *Alif Laila* (One Thousand and One Nights) in Urdu from the right to left; access to the lexical spectrum of the Indo-Aryan as well as Abrahamic civilizations, is the beginning of a lifelong curiosity about the ancient trade routes named the Silk Road, Peshawar itself being an outpost, and *Qissa khani* bazaar (or "market of the storytellers"), its relic. It'll be many years until I'll actually visit the area many of the stories conjure— Central Asia— as a grownup and a writer.

Ay Pari, O Fairy!

In Tian Shan mountains of the legendary snow leopard, errant wisps of mist float with the speed of scurrying ghosts, there is a climbers' cemetery, Himalayan Griffin vultures and golden eagles are often sighted, though my attention is completely arrested by a Blue whistling thrush alighting on a rock— its plumage, its slender, seemingly weightless frame, and its long drawn, ventriloquist song remind me of the fairies of *Alif Laila* that were turned to birds by demons inhabiting barren mountains.

The sense of enchantment is powerful and not entirely unexpected. "Ay Pari" (O Fairy!), sung by the *Badakhsan Ensemble,* I imagine as a song sung in a human language in response to the eloquent whistle of the thrush, really a fairy under a spell. The word "fairy" in English may have been derived from the ancient Zoroastrian Persian "pari:" the first mythic creature I remember from lore and lullabies and the television show *Alif Laila* (Arabian Nights) in Urdu. The song, in an eastern Persian dialect, comes from the heart of the Pamir mountains— the range that not only joins the Tian Shan in Kyrgyzstan to the north, and to the south, borders the Hindukush, the mountains of my childhood in Pakistan. The Pamirs are also the source of the famed river Oxus or Amu Darya—the drainage area of which was once the space between the empire of Genghis Khan, and over a thousand years earlier, of Alexander the Great. Classical Persian poetry and literature amply mythologize and illustrate the drama of empire that took place in these regions, and some of these artistic/literary masterpieces sparked the imagination of Victorian poets such as Mathew Arnold who describes the river Oxus in his poem *Sohrab and Rustam:*

Oxus, forgetting the bright speed he had
In his high mountain-cradle in Pamere,
A foiled circuitous wanderer: — till at last
The longed-for dash of waves is heard, and wide
His luminous home of waters opens, bright
And tranquil, from whose floor the new-bathed stars
Emerge, and shine upon the Aral Sea.

Urdu, my mother tongue, is a child of many parents; its lexical richness borne of diverse cultures carried along the Silk Roads crisscrossing the Pamirs— trading, warring, marrying, exchanging influences in art, music, spirituality, poetry, cuisine and the mythic imagination.

I speak about these influences on Urdu and the Ghazal form, as I read passages from my book *Ghazal Cosmopolitan* at the American University of Central Asia, at an event that is part of the reason I find myself here in Kyrgyzstan. The young women organizers of my book event are bright and engaging— they belong to the generation of Afghans whose parents were children during the Soviet War, my generation, the displaced generation that I write poems about; my work, I hear, has been part of the literature course at AUCA, taught by the American poet Raphael Dagold. I feel an affinity with these students— they are sensitive but untouched by cynicism, the faces of a future I could not have predicted during the many traumatic decades of recent Afghan history.

During my brief stay in Bishkek, I have the finest host and companion possible— Haniya Tirmizi, wife of Faisal Tirmizi, the Pakistani ambassador to Kyrgistan— who weaves in and out of English, Russian and Urdu, as we walk through Osh bazaar, my first actual experience of what I have imagined a Silk Road marketplace to be like (selling "An assortment of crooked/ and straight arrows/for the crest of a bulbul/ or a handful of sesame," lines from my poem "Trade").

A Silk Road Bazaar

I hunger for the spontaneous theater that a bazaar is— in the rising and falling rhythms of bargaining, banter, vendor songs, the strategic, pleasing arrangement of goods, the feasts of colors and aromas, there is an underlying confluence of art and trade, a tension between spirit, form, purpose, and value, much like the making of a poem. No other marketplace showcased the wares of more abundant and diverse cultures than the bazars of the ancient Silk Roads, the network of trading routes across some of the oldest civilizations. If Istanbul's Grand Bazaar is a taste of the old marketplace built on a massive scale, one that has preserved its imperial refinement and continues to modify itself, Osh bazaar feels like a labyrinthine, other-worldly place where *Saum*, the currency used, has a denomination of three, the figure of magic spells.

In these final days of autumn, there is a thrill in the cool, golden sunshine; the air has an unmistakable alpine crispness. We buy felt caps and tea-cozies with embroidery, bread with floral designs. "Kishmish" (sultana raisins) and all manner of nuts, spices, teas, and fruits heaped on carts in Osh bazar, or displayed in Bishkek supermarkets evoke scenes from stories of childhood: *One Thousand and One Nights*, *Qissa-e-Chahar Darwish*, *Amir Hamza*; also, narratives of the Great Game, a geopolitical intrigue involving massive swathes of fuel- and mineral-rich lands in Asia, the control over which began with the spice- and tea-trade a few centuries ago.

By the Ak-Sai River

Ascending the Ala Archa National Park, we sense a wintry desolation. Haniya's garden which was a festival of roses in honeyed sunlight this morning, would be covered in deep snow only two days later. I see the Ak-Sai river, which flows with a melting glacier as its source. I hear of trout. Just when we reach the top and I take quick strides to see a yurt in real life, it begins to snow; I open my mouth to take in some Central Asian flurry. The mini "foyer" and simple threshold of the yurt give no clue to the festive interior, even more magical when seen through the crack of a locked door.

In the juniper forests that the Ala Archa Park is named after, wild goats, deer, and even snow leopards are spotted. I see none of these animals, but my heart skips a beat when I see the famed Central Asian horses—they are as sleek as the numerous depictions I have seen in miniatures and paintings in museums. I enjoy sharing some of the excitement of my visit with my illustrious dinner hosts Sohail and Iram Naqvi, sharing "Ghazal for the Girl in the Photo," which I wrote for Sharbat Gula whose suffering, relatable because of my childhood memory of Afghan refugees in Peshawar, may be called a casualty of the Great Game.

Leaving this land of legends and losses, the song of the native blue whistling thrush becomes doubly haunting as it combines with the loveliness of an Urdu song Haniya sings on our drive down from Ala Archa. A song, not for a fairy but for a loved one soon to be married— this song, both in diction and melody, is a shiny thread of the intricate, tightly woven cultures of the Silk Road.

Wishing to know where the River Indos emptied itself

"Wishing to know where the River Indos emptied itself into the sea, he (King Darius of Persia) sent a number of men… among them Skulax of Karuanda, to sail down the river. They started from the city of Kaspaturos (Peshawar) and the country of Paktuke, and sailed down the river to the east and the sunrise to the sea."

Herodotus
Book 4, 44, 486-420 BCE

Crowns at a Crossroads

A shock of unruly hair, curls tumbling down his neck. Heavy lips with a suggestive cast under a straight, immodest nose running directly into a prominent brow, his head set in its characteristic leftward tilt.

This is how historian Paddy Docherty describes the stone bust of Alexander the Great in the British Museum, in his book *The Khyber Pass: A History of Empire and Invasion*— a work that looks at Peshawar, valley of my childhood, as a momentous crossroads between the East and the West. The relic in Docherty's description is originally from Alexandria, Egypt.

Among the dozen or so "Alexandrias" – cities that Alexander founded in the lands he conquered—several exist in the farthest reaches of his empire in the East, in what are now Afghanistan and Pakistan. One of these cities, Alexandria Bucephalous, on river Jehlum in Punjab, east of the Indus is named after Alexander's lifelong companion, his beloved horse Bucephalous. Though Alexander defeated his Indian adversary Porus, this attack was to be the final of his long series of military offensives across the world; the Macedonian prince, famed victor, died soon after his return to Babylon, some say from poisoning, others, from the gradual weakening effects of the wounds he suffered in the battle of Hydaspes (Jehlum) in present-day Pakistan.

The story of Alexander and Bucephalous as I know it, doesn't end with the historic burial of the beloved horse and the master's grief and subsequent death; it continues from the moment both Alexander and Bucephalous are struck in battle. They pass on to a purgatory of sorts, searching for the healing water, the "aab e hayat" or "fountain of life" to recover from the mortal wounds. The desperate search leads Alexander to engage with Khizer, the immortal saint and sage, the only one to have drunk from the miraculous fountain. The journey turns into a spiritual quest—Khizer teaches "Zulqarnain," as Alexander is known in legends of the Muslim world— to shatter the illusion of worldly power through introspection, and imbibe the true purpose of life rather than to insist on the thirst for immortality.

At the MET Museum in New York, I linger by the Persian art depicting Alexander in illuminated manuscripts of the *Shahnameh*, the Book of Kings. Theorized by many commentators to be the prophet *Dhul Qarnain* (Zulqarnain) the "two-horned one," mentioned in the Qura'an as well as in earlier Abrahamic texts, recognized as Alexander the Great or *Iskandar e Azam*, in pre-Islamic Persian, *Iskander al Akbar* in Arabic, Sikander in the vernacular, he is a figure embedded in legends that intersect and thread through traditions as diverse and intertwined as the peoples he conquered— from Gibralter to the Punjab—covering Asia Minor, the Levant, Syria, Egypt, Assyria, Babylonia, Persia, Media, Parthia, Scythia, Bactria and parts of the subcontinent. Of Persian visage and dress in some versions, his portrayals in the East assume a more and more complex language as the influence of Chinese and Western aesthetics are added to the mix during the later Ilkhanid (or Muslim Mongol) period. Alexander appears in other sections of the museum mostly in Greek garb, war ready.

The chapter that marks the beginning of the end of Alexander's life, his last conquest, takes place very close to Peshawar, the Khyber Pass. Docherty describes the entry of Alexander's army in these words: "At the narrow confine by Ali Masjid, where the Khyber closes to just feet in width, the army would have squeezed through, two or three abreast, looking up warily at the steep heights immediately above them; unknown creatures might inhabit these mountains, for assuredly, India was full of wonders." Millennia later, another force from Europe, the British, will enter with the same awe of India, though by a different route, and relying more on economic and political strategy than military— meeting their most challenging adversary in precisely these parts, the Westernmost outpost of their empire in the subcontinent.

Alexander's fondness, as emperor, for donning the Persian dress, will find an echo in Britain's romance with the culture of the subcontinent. In *White Mughals*, William Dalrymple describes a painting with the following caption: "At a Lucknow dinner party c.1820. The gentleman at the head of the table smokes his hookah and wears a Lucknavi jama over his British military uniform." The adoption of oriental ways proved to be a dalliance for the British in the long run, whereas Alexander, at the height of his power, married a princess of Persian blood, choosing her over a potential bride of Macedonian or Greek nobility. Quintus Citrius Rufus, a Roman historian drawing from Greek accounts of the time, mentions in his work *The History of Alexander*, that Alexander spoke of uniting Europe and Asia into one kingdom, and that he sought "to erase all distinction between conquered and conqueror." Was he earnest in his intentions? Was the bloodbath forgiven by so many of his former enemies on the grounds that he really was fighting oppression and was successful in establishing a just reign, opposing even his mentor, the great Aristotle, who, for all his fabled wisdom, reinforced the prevalent belief that the Greeks were superior to non-Greeks— that the "Barbarians" deserved less? How could one so young win a series of expeditions in the world's most powerful territories in such a short time, planting the roots of Hellenism and making a lasting impact by linking disparate civilizations from the East to the West— most importantly, how could a colonizer become mythologized by subjugated cultures as a sage, a warrior of superhuman qualities, a philosopher, a deity, an ideal ruler, regarded as a saint or prophet?

When I see Alexander's statue for the first time, I am around seven or eight and have read a Ladybird Series book about him. His story presents him as an enigma, even at my age, but the assortment of artifacts from distinct civilizations coming together in Peshawar's museum is a bigger enigma; the collection reflects a history that would take many lifetimes to comprehend and piece together as the story of a single place. I find that the man whose likenesses, in the Greek style, dominate this museum is not Alexander, but another prince, who, like Alexander, left home and changed the world. Preceding Alexander likely by some two hundred years, his name is Siddhartha Gautama, known commonly as the Buddha, and said to have come, not with armed men or a royal entourage, but alone— an ascetic with a begging bowl— followed, not by another wave of generals and rulers hundreds of years later from the West, but by pilgrims from the East.

This very land, the ancient Peshawar basin, with Indus to the east, Sulayman mountains to the west, the confluence of rivers Kabul and Swat at its center, was the home of the Gandhara civilization, which coalesced, among others, the two very different worlds that Alexander and Buddha represent. So many epochs have entwined themselves with this place, I wonder at the allure of this air, my ordinary breath; I wonder what magnets of earthly or spiritual energy have pulled such varied populations to this soil.

Within the radius of a few miles, one encounters the signs of the city's Hindu, Buddhist, Persian, Greek, Muslim and British past. Mentioned in the ancient text *Rigveda* (c.1500-c.1200), and later, the *Avesta*, Gandahara was a land that was said to be the sixth most beautiful place created by the deity Ahura Mazda of the early Zoroastrian tradition. The Persian Achaemenid empire took Gandhara in the sixth century BC— the period when Buddha is said to have lived. It is ironic that both Buddha and Alexander would not only have Peshawar in common but also the Persians, whose influence over India never ceased. Docehrty writes: "Iran gave India many political and administrative ideas, a corpus of important literature, expertise in metalwork and architecture, along with techniques of building in stone. In later years, stimuli from the sophisticated urban culture of Iran—more cosmopolitan than its Hindu neighbor—were essential fillips to Indian development; the Khyber Pass was the essential means of transmission. That the exchange was freely welcomed by both sides is undoubted: Persian was to become the language of government and the elite under the Muslim rulers of India from 1000 A.D, who quite naturally embraced whatever came from Iran. It is a compelling thought that the body of literature written in India in the Persian language during the medieval and early modern period vastly outweighs that composed in Iran itself."

Buddha is conjectured to have visited Peshawar and meditated under a pipal tree that became a sacred site for pilgrims through the centuries. According to Dr. Amjad Hussain, who has done extensive work on Peshawar's archeological and cultural history: "A relic casket in gilt bronze was recovered containing Buddha's bone fragments and ashes" in excavations carried out in 1911. The casket is found in the writings of antiquity, mentioned by Chinese pilgrims who visited Gandhara. It is curious that the followers of one who surrendered the riches he was born into, seeking the purpose of life through asceticism, would preserve his remains in a gilded casket. Alexander, in contrast, is said to have instructed his men before his death, to open his fists, palms facing up, for all at the funeral to see that the world's greatest conqueror was leaving it empty-handed.

Alexander claimed Gandhara in 327 BC and departed. The subsequent rule of the Maurian empire established Gandhara as the center of Buddhism, to be cultivated by the later Kushan empire of Bactria, and under the Hellenistic rule of the Indo-Greek kingdom that followed, further nurturing the tradition of Gandharan Buddhism, which was passed on especially through the art of sculpture, a quintessential Greco-Roman art that traveled East and West and left a lasting impression. In the post-Kushan period, according to Dr. Amjad Hussain, in his book *The Frontier Town of Peshawar: A Brief History*: "for a thousand years thereafter, a string of invaders came to the Peshawar Valley. The Huns (455-550 AD) were followed by the Sassanians, Saffavids, Ghaznavids, Ghorids, and Seljuk Turks from Ghazni. In 1220 AD, the Mongol king Genghis Khan, looted the valley and later his descendants, the Timurids (notable among them Tamarlane), ruled the region including Punjab and Delhi." Following this conquest, Peshawar would fall under Mughal, Sikh, and British rule, before becoming part of Pakistan in 1947. It was in the time of British India, in 1893, that the demarcation of Afghanistan's border took place— "until then, the kings of Kabul considered the territory west of the Indus as their domain and the people were called Pakhtuns or Afghans. After the boundary demarcation, the people east of the border in present day Pakistan were called Pakhtuns, whereas their western cousins in Afghanistan were called Afghans"— explains Dr. Amjad Hussain.

At the Peshawar museum, I see an astonishing array of Gandharan art; I'm particularly taken by the friezes that tell a story, such as the scene of Buddha's birth or death. The visual art of religious biography is an unfamiliar concept for me, but I am enthralled by the elaborate devotional expressions of different traditions, converging and diverging.

The architecture of the Peshawar Museum itself reflects Peshawar Valley's mixed heritage. Built in 1907 by the British in the subcontinental syncretic style, fusing the British Raj sensibility with the Mughal Islamic, Buddhist, and Hindu style, and named "Victoria Hall" after the sovereign of the time, Queen Victoria, it is a ruddy building, the pinkish tones of which, in my memory, are set off by deep green cypresses, palm trees and maybe rosebushes. The Peshawar museum has changed over the years, since I frequented it. It is now said to house 14,000 artifacts of Gandhara, the largest collection in the world. Besides the Greco-Bactrian, it houses Persian, Mughal, Kailash, tribal Pukhtun, and British items.

As a child, I find this dimly lit, often cold and quiet place true to its name—"ajaaib ghar" or museum. The etymology of the phrase, "house of wonders," in Urdu's hybrid vocabulary evokes the sense of disparate strands coming together – "ajaib" plural of "ajeeb" or "a marvel" or "strange" in Arabic and "ghar" (ger) meaning "house" in Mongol. It is a marvel indeed that Alexander, the ultimate signifier of Western civilization is glorified in the artistic and literary traditions of the East, and Buddha, very much a symbol of the East, is celebrated most famously in the Western-influenced art of Gandhara.

Images of heroes and gods inevitably mirror the makers; the Indian Buddha wears a loincloth, has a large forehead, a distinctive brow-bone, flared nostrils, large eyes, curly hair— the Greek Buddha has features that are recognizable as classic Greek features—he's relatively slender, muscled, sometimes with almost athletic proportions, a regal bone structure. Perhaps, like Alexander, the Buddha appears to have an "immodest nose" and like Alexander, he is depicted in a toga, a prince with no crown, but unlike Alexander, there are no unruly curls or battle helmet— Buddha wears his hair gathered neatly at the top.

The Comb Engraved with a Battle Scene

has nineteen fine teeth
and five fully formed lions
squeezed between two bars of solid gold

Empire, having struck the lions
feeble as rotten gourds,
uses their hunched ferocity as a vignette

to frame a scene ripe for violence:

a cavalier about to drive a spear into the enemy
whose shield is more like a harp
(filled with song fractures
for future gnawing)
whose fallen horse with upturned legs
(is a baby I want to cradle)
four bent legs of pure gold
will flail atop a wealthy woman's head
as she smooths her curls in the looking glass

The Legend of Khizer

The camera, on the roof of a teashop, was abandoned for two reasons:

In the winter mist of a Persian garden, the camera had caught a green-cloaked figure.

Then, at the moment a village lorry belched, tearing the song of a snow finch into confetti, there were five seconds of static on the camera before it ran out of battery.

Khizer — the "green one," the wise, the longest-living saint of the road— is nearly impossible to pursue. I know that but I try. Often I'm woken up by the image of Khizer and the fur that shimmers green with him. What follows is an elusive map plotting the mornings I have lived and the ones yet to live. Mortality's math is a fur map that smothers, so I rise and wander— the house, the street, land and sea.

And by wandering, rub against the possible particles of an answer— salts of the land are pounded desire, salts of the sea melt desire into shape. Between them, a green curtain that lifts and carries you into peace as if it were the planet's mighty sail.

When the abrasions of the quest cool, I hear a footfall in the clock of my mortality. It is Khizer's, who drank from the fountain of life to become the traveling sage, the saint of the lost. The metaphors are more real than me, and Khizer, a man of quest, is of common proportions and immeasurable grace.

I look for him in library lobbies, bazars, cafes, festivals and conferences, on ferries and trains— all desolate places. Mortality's helmeted shadow lengthens on my door. I recall that

Alexander the Great wanted to conquer death after he had conquered the world. More fixed on finding the elixir of life than recognizing the journey itself as the elixir, he lost his way. When he lay dying he told his men to open his palms for all to see that he was leaving empty-handed. Khizer found the ancient fountain *Aab e hayaat* while quietly helping other children of the road find themselves. To get to the rest of the story, you must slowly climb the rickety ladder of wisdom.

The ladder is made of millions of weak magnets. I have yet to reach it but I hear the magnets are the voices of elders— the same voices we become adept at subduing.

The lorry has brought tourists to the teashop. Some are here for tea and sweets, some will buy postcards of the garden and pet the cats. Some know they are lost. They will keep their ear to the wall for broken songs, and strain to see through the mist.

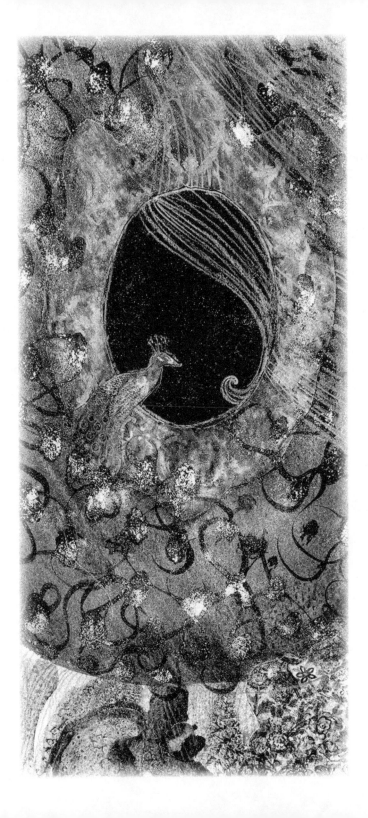

Wedding Combs

Out of the hundred clove-scented
fine-spun braids in the bride's hair
How many
       will the groom unravel?

A wedding night on this mountain
rings with the clangor of the womenfolk—
gilt-edged, tassel-tied, prismatic—

Look
       the tatters in the velvet of lunar light
       Her new entwined life
       Knots to open every night

Until our hair becomes white
A vow on a different mountain
is exchanged with a gift of combs
       carved of Mahogany and completed
       in seventy-two steps

And while God swears by epochs
we are fathomed
by the gauze of a single autumn
       half the susurrus between the wings
       of a Himalayan bulbul

Less with each combing

Henna Night, Hair Jewels

I choose MC Escher's geometric drawing of a flock of inter-locked birds, printed in golden ink, for my wedding invita-tion card because these birds appear to me to form a webbed nest while in flight, wings raised; what a stupendous task to make a home of abeyance, weaving themselves as they do, into eternity— a metaphor for the sharing of mortality's burden and paradox of permanence in flux. Marriage locks not only a man and a woman but both their past and future families, the entire, impossible flock, into confluence, a slowed, synchro-nous flight whose grace comes with its own aches. Shameem, the one I've decided at age twenty-two, to marry, is sensitive and brilliant; a friend of my brother's from Caltech days, a rare science guy who has an ear for poetry, and some of whose quirks (such as singing jingles from TV ads) are uncannily like mine. At twenty-six, he seems to have the strength, bal-ance, humor, patience and talent for the synchronicity neces-sary. But of course, only time will tell.

On a foggy December morning, I have my *nikah* ceremony, a brief prayer and signing of wedding contracts, at home, in Peshawar, surrounded by family and friends visiting from across the country and from three different continents; I wear a pearl-colored sari with a golden border and ask my cousin Sadia to wrap my hair with the strings of fresh jas-mines my mother-in-law has brought with a lovingly assem-bled trousseau. Over the years, Mama, as everyone calls Shameem's mother (even her own mother-in-law) and I will bond over many things we love, flowers among them. Mama is a transplant from Germany; she met Papa, a PhD student from Karachi in Berlin where they both studied Physics. Her name, Margrit, is the name of a flower, as I learn on a visit to Nathiagali resort in the mountains where my parents invite her to plan the wedding; the joy that the "margrits" blooming wild on the hillside bring her, resonates with me; her disposition is familiar.

It strikes me, as I think of marriage and moving away, that Ami too, is a transplant, though not from another continent; she is part-Kashmiri, part- Multani, both places known as lands of the Sufis. Ami has a way of making us a home within the present moment, a sanctuary cobbled out of the voice of love any place we might find ourselves on the planet. I learn from Ami and Mama that nostalgia is a living thing, and the memories of places past must be nurtured, that our purpose, as women, is to braid and bind time with family, and the places we call home, will become a reality woven as a continuum of love.

There are not enough days, in the six months between engagement and marriage, to comb through memories and orient myself in the in-between-ness.

My parents host the henna party at Peshawar's Pearl Continental Hotel. It's a chilly, cloudy day outside; inside, the air is excited with dressy perfume, music, lights, roses and chatter. My outfit for the henna night is a silk *kuchi* dress tailored in a facility for Afghan refugees; my hair is braided with flowers and I wear a chiffon veil and a pearl-studded cap with Afghan embroidery. Shameem wears an ivory raw silk *kurta shalwar* and lapis lazuli cuff links that my mother has designed; we see each other as a married couple for the first time. I decide to keep my face veiled until the more formal bridal ceremony on the following day, the occasion of "rukhsati" or departure of the bride with the groom and his family. This is an unusual choice; brides of my generation don't wear a face veil. As always, my parents accept my whim.

The henna ceremony, with all its bursts of music, color and festive chaos will leave the most articulate trail of having been loved through my early years. I suddenly feel lonely in this moment which lands like childhood's grand finale. Every face here carries a trace of my life's essence thus far, in every laugh there's a tiny mirror. Cousins and friends will carry henna in glittered clay bowls dotted with small, lit candles; they'll sing as they walk in procession, raising a canopy of a bridal *dupatta* over me. My aunts arrange and shepherd the procession, re-lighting candles that go out, tucking away parts of garments close enough to catch fire. There is singing and dancing and banter between the bride- and groom-sides. Sweets are arsenal in our wedding customs. Saleem, my brother-in-law, sabotages Nomi by stuffing a whole *laddu* in his mouth; more *laddu* fights ensue. Many years later, visiting Karachi to help prepare for Saleem and Ghazala's wedding, I'd recall this time.

On our wedding day, Shameem arrives in an elegant *sherwani* and turban; his green eyes have a fire in them and his smile is generous, as always. I wear the bridal regalia Ami has put together, including the gold and ruby "tika," a hair jewel that is pinned atop and dangles on the forehead. I wear some of her bridal jewelry but my outfit is a traditional red and golden *gharara* whereas hers had been a shade of pink fashionable at the time of her marriage. On my drive to the Pearl, I turn to look at the mountains one last time in the winter dusk, hoping to lock in the scenes along the great Jamrud:

One of my earliest ghazals captures the bride's farewell:

They said, "a fistful of rice!" Instead, I threw a glance
over my shoulder at the thin copper mist, at my city diluting.

Everything was in need of a bride's blessing: forts, schools,
buses, stationery shops, even the Indus in the distance, diluting.

My dowry was a silk cap with geometrically broken hearts,
sewn by Afghan refugees; in art's labor, their grief diluting.

A cap lined with Rumi's verses must find the poet-bride.
But all it found was a yellowed dream, its memory diluting.

Look, the calm of the yogurt sellers, magazine vendors
before the bomb-blast, and afterwards, all peace diluting.

Do not forget, Zeest, the green-guava scent of this town or
the beauty of labor, as your groom sees your henna diluting.

I'm visiting Peshawar for the wedding, after having been
away since I turned sixteen. Between now and the time I left
home to attend Kinnaird in Lahore and later Reed College
in America, I'm smack in the middle of two wars across the
border in Afghanistan; the Soviet War, the war of my childhood, and the American war, the war through which I would
raise my children, though the view of Safed koh mountains
visible from the window on our *Nikah* day will be the last
and I'll happen to return to it as a family only once, when
Shameem and I return from San Diego and visit Peshawar
for two days with our first-born Yaseen as an infant. The
only other time I catch a brief glimpse of the outskirts of the
city is at Nomi's wedding— my sister in law Laila belongs to
Peshawar. The boys are aged nine and seven years and the
baby is ten months old at the time— I find myself with only
a few precious moments to show them a glimpse or two of
the city:

I almost say to you,
Look out the window,
look, look, look!
My library with beetle-eaten furniture,
my raw silk bazaar, my ancient fort!
And look, the bakery that sells pink coconut rolls!
And look, there I used to get my haircut.

One turn and my town will once again
socket into its timeless hollow
what I remember, what I know.
The bus will pass
all these things
before you click pause on your video game.

20th Wedding Anniversary

Damascene Hairpin

Gibraltar in the background, I pose sideways, wearing a Spanish Chrysanthemum claw in my hair, *gitana* style, taking a dare from my husband. The photo is from an August afternoon, captured in the sun's manic glare. My shadow in profile, with the oversized flower behind my ear, mirrors the shape of Gibraltar, *Jabl ut Tariq* or "Tariq's rock." On this, my second visit to Spain, I'm hearing the rock more clearly though it'll take another decade and a half until I actually visit this piece of British overseas territory attached to Iberia. What it says to me is that erased history is no different from the poet's skin, thinned, yet enduring, feeding on enigma.

On our first visit to Spain in 1996, we take the train from Barcelona to Cordoba and I see Andalucia, the fabled al-Andalus for the first time. The sunshine is rapturous but it is January and there is a nip in the air. My husband is astonished at my choice of outfit; I wear my knit woolen *shalwar kameez*, swede boots, leather bolero jacket and a velvet cap with Afghan embroidery. He thinks I'm eccentric but I find a sense of coherence and comfort in mixing apparel of different cultures. The life of syncretic sensibilities I have lived is unexamined thus far, but desire is wont to appear on the sleeve before it morphs into an intellectual preoccupation. I will spend the rest of my life trying to explore cultures of encounter— Al Andalus being the first one.

Somnambulant, the spirit of Al Andalus roams the streets by night. It is dressed as a poem, a thing of ancient assemblage and modern alacrity, a bewilderingly familiar thing. The street I'm on, one of Cordoba's oldest, is so narrow that if the wall across from me were a looking glass, a puff of my breath would fog it. It is terrifying in the way a sudden mirror in a labyrinth is terrifying; I am encased in an

infinity of reflections, meandering through this neighborhood of timelessness which was made known to me first in
the early twentieth century Urdu poem "Masjid-e-Qurtu-
ba" ("The Mosque of Cordoba") by Iqbal, then in a concert
of music from three distinct Abrahamic traditions played
by the Al Andalus Ensemble at Reed College, my alma
mater – insinuations leading me to reunite with a crowd
of Andalusi ghosts I have always known, and which, years
from now, I will recall:

*And so windows crack open. Under streetlights, ancient faces are em-
bedded in pillars. Sketched in rust they bleed into each other. These
ghosts of Al Andalus come on rich wafts of tannin ink and pomegranate pulp, poised between oud strings – vibrato of a dream. They leap
from a basin of mercury to the high, filigreed domes...*

*Some have a furtive way of surfacing in a note of the ney flute, slip-
ping ever so lightly into the seam joining two breaths, while others
place themselves stubbornly on my patio ledge in California, legs dan-
gling, refusing to leave until I hear them out.*

*They are scribes and stonemasons, merchants, seamstresses, philoso-
phers, gardeners and governors.*

Al Andalus will haunt me permanently in dreams, but it is
not a dreamscape; it is a gritty world of paradox, a question,
an answer couched in a life-affirming, creative energy.

On the flight from Karachi to Frankfurt, before the train
trip through Europe, I'm in my silk *shalwar kameez* and
high heels. I am a young newlywed: halved, doubled, but
protean, wearing a new identity I have not yet divined or
defined. Having grown up in the "East" and finished my
education in the "West," I am on a cusp of identities. I have
left behind many places I call home, each bordering with
another country: Lahore, my birthplace on the border with

India; Peshawar, my hometown, with Afghanistan; Portland where I attended college, in the Northwestern United States, the vicinity of the Canadian border. My future home, the city I will live in the longest, is San Diego, along the border with Mexico.

I don't know it yet, on my first visit to Cordoba, but I'm inside the tremor of exile— the primeval, paramount home of poetry. I am drawn to the world of Al Andalus because it is a gift of exiles, a celebration of the cusp, of plural identities, the meeting point of three continents and three faiths, where the drama of boundaries and their blurring took place. I will soon discover that the father of Al Andalus, the Umayyad prince Abd al Rahman (731—788) was himself an exile and a poet, and that before he built the arches that open out as a great forest of palms in the Mosque of Cordoba, an 8th-century architectural wonder which was arguably the first modern building in Europe, he planted what happened to be the first palm in Europe (in his palace named *Rusafa*) and wrote a poem in memory of his home, Rusafa, in Syria: "A palm tree I beheld in Ar-Rusafa,/Far in the West/far from the palm-tree land:/I said: You, like myself, are far away, in a strange land." I will find this Arabic poem translated into English, in my search for Andalusi poetry; later I will be fascinated to discover Iqbal's Urdu adaptation of this very poem in his collected works, *Kuliyaat-e-Iqbal*. Abd al Rahman, the homesick poet-prince from Damascus, brought such powerful beauty to the Western world— a legacy that ultimately triumphed against the worst forms of erasure. A Damascene hairpin from Toledo, Spain, marks the page of his poem in Iqbal's book; It is a reminder.

In the coming years, I piece it all together as I respond to my new place as an immigrant in America and consider from a distance what my Muslim forbears may have experienced in pre-partition India, through their migration to Pakistan: the country of desire, the country of reality.

On this winter day in 1996, Spain is true to its promise of sunshine. From my balcony, I catch a glimpse of an abandoned scooter in the narrow street down below; a dove rests on it. *In the milky light, with traces of rain only in the scent of the earth, this bird could be the one Noah sent to find out whether the world was habitable. It stirs at the sound of schoolchildren and hops on to the wall of the synagogue. The day sweet and filled with light, it glides over the dome of the mosque. In the patio of oranges, there are fountains for ablution. It drinks the water, leaves the patio glistening like a worshipper. There are memories of a nest here. It flies to the enormous bell of the cathedral in the lungs of the mosque. Broken feathers float in the gilded emptiness, the chapel agape.*

I see feathers cut by the blades of a tyranny that is startlingly out of place in this air. I see a dispersal of light, its evenhanded promise, then I see a violent blockage — both, as figured in history and as the literal fact of my visit to the "Mezquita," Mosque turned museum, where it is forbidden to pray, whereas the cathedral, built inside the mosque's original structure, is a functioning worship-place. The forest of columns, a metaphor for infinity, carries an emotive sense of abundance as well as a subtle anonymity/autonomy that promotes private meditation; any point under the grove of arches can become the center, liberating the viewer from a forced, predetermined center. But this original design of the mosque was rendered meaningless as its delicacy, continuity and light were cut off by the installation of a cathedral in the 13th century and its subsequent expansion in the 16th century— an overbearing, massively gilded, permanent interruption to the fluidity of spiritual desire that Iqbal praises in his poem 'Masjid-e-Qurtaba;" it crosses the fine line between abundance and excess, ambition and hubris, art and artifice.

The day I visit the Mezquita there are few visitors. The guard offers to turn the lights on only in the spaces we find ourselves in — I am petrified and will not fathom my fear for years to come, and for this reason, I will start a book of poems. As I navigate the large building I have really fallen into an ocean, and I am desperately swimming against a gigantic tide of darkness. This will be a recurring dream for long, starting tonight — its unsettling force will sustain the drive to write my first poetry collection, *Baker of Tarifa*, over the next decade and a half.

I walk by the Guadalquivir, river of epic beauty; we take photographs on the Roman bridge. I leave Cordoba in a few days but I am tethered. Before long, I will return to my ghosts: *Of the two bestirred, sleepless nights, the first was spent in Cordoba's Juderia, yards away from the Mezquita-Catedral where the streets are narrow as capillaries. And the second was in the Alhambra where my room was a whisper away from the Rauda, the royal graveyard of the Nasrids.*

On a starry night in 2004, I will lie on a stone bench a few steps from the Nasrid palace in the Alhambra. Among all the ghosts I meet here, the most compelling one will be the ghost of the last Muslim empress, the Morayma, wife of Boabdil, the "Moor of the last sigh"; she will figure in many of my poems and will come to embody the tragic end of Al Andalus: *Eight hundred years have passed in Al Andalus, Muslim Spain — years turning like great mills, a resplendence of work reflected in books and buildings, cities and institutions, technology and aesthetics, bridging antiquity with modernity, east with west, fissured periodically but sewn back again and again by Iberian Muslims, Jews and Christians. Al Andalus, which, under Muslim rule, has brought about a transformation simply through inter-translation, which has dared to find direction in deviation from the known and accepted, where the Abrahamic people have found enough peace to transcend literalism and worship willingly in each other's sacred places, to inscribe the other's scripture on their own walls, is collapsing. All that signifies Al Andalus — the books, maps, machines, manuals, poetry, medical and musical instruments, recipes, calligraphy — is about to be destroyed forever; a near-millennium of civilization utterly wiped out by the crushing machinery of the Inquisition; a tyranny of epic proportions poised to swallow an epic legacy of tolerance. It is the year that Morayma's fate becomes knotted with the fate of the last Andalusi bastion, Granada.*

Here, in Granada, I will imagine Al Andalus in the throes of the brutal inquisition most vividly. I will also find the work of the 20th-century Spanish poet Federico Garcia Lorca as I learn about Al Andalus and its rebirths in poetry. Lorca, who was a native of Granada and had fallen under the spell of Andalusi history and culture, gave a modern reinterpretation – stylistic and thematic – of Al Andalus. I will be fascinated by his "gacelas" (ghazals) and "casidas" (qasidas), forms I know well from my study of Urdu literature, and which he wrote as a way to enter an erased, haunting, invigorating past whose mystique and poetic sensibility he identified with and felt the urgency to express. Lorca's work was produced at a time when, according to a contemporary of Lorca's, Europe was "suffering from a withering of the ability to desire." A recurrent word in Lorca's poetry is "quiero" or "I desire," and in Robert Bly's words, Lorca "adopted old Arab forms to help entangle that union of desire and darkness, which the ancient Arabs loved so much." Lorca's Andalucia-inspired theory of *duende* or "desire-energy" will validate my initial response to the restless but vivifying spirits of the place, and confirm the haunting power of Al Andalus.

Back in San Diego, I will "fight a duel on the rim of a well" with *duende*, as Lorca describes it, striking for art-giving life and life-giving art, as I balance parenting with writing. My research over the next decade will prove to be rewarding. I will discover facts about the history of Al Andalus, facts that make natural bridges of metaphors. For example, sugar, one of the multitudinous gifts of Al Andalus to Europe, will lead to a chorus of bakers—my poem set in the confectioners' district of Sevilla, and another poem in the voice of a monk making marzipan roses in a monastery. The image of sugar and paper (which is probably the greatest gift of Al Andalus) will prompt me to mine childhood memories of seeing paper being made from sugarcane husk in Pakistan (at a paper mill right next to a sugar mill in the district of Charsada) and to recast them as I craft a scribe's dream in which she is visited by a jinn (a word related to *genius* in Latin) in a sugarcane field, where she is inspired to create paper out of sugarcane husk instead of the commonly-used linen. Through a dream, I will bind a persona to a future time and a foreign place where her dream is realized:

When their eyes locked
she saw paper

acres
of sweet milled paper

The field had melted
from green to copper
pulp to gauze

A hush was falling

She bolted from the gaze
Upset her inkpot

A rich black
soaked
through the chewed up cane
stain of cynosure
on the day's lost wages

Writing narrative, prose, and persona poems that contain actual authors and thinkers of the period, fictional scribes, bookbinders and mapmakers, I will revel in making utopic imagery of Al Andalus's culture of libraries. I will recreate scenes with calligraphers, kilns baking tiles, recipes for bread, and the *furn* (communal ovens where Muslims, Jews and Christians brought their dough), and with these I will string a chain of poems about book-burning pyres, and the congregations, not of bakers but people forced to watch the spectacle of their own ethnic cleansing carried out by the engineers of the Inquisition:

Window in La Madraza
Granada: 1499

In the University
Rooms echo with the pounding
One last ache
For anything that was ever dear

This is how death begins
The soldiers use rope
To tie five or six heavy ones
Ten or twelve light

Years though only a few hundred
This scent of tannin and reed remains
Of the scribe and the reader
Scent of words over and over

And above
The funeral pyre of books
Rise memories of the paper that was linen
Made into pages one at a time

Meaning left in the powder of ash
The soot on the cheeks
Of the soldiers
And the grieving ones

In the absence of research materials early on in my work, I will come to rely heavily on art, and especially the music of the period, writing only while listening. Andalusi musical compositions, as well as the destruction of instruments and written music, will be a recurring theme:

When the spell broke

Ziryab's lute strings
were strewn like intestines of stray animals

Carved wood ceilings had turned
into snuff-boxes

Galleries were sweating paint

On the walnut shelves
Corpses with coins

Groves cut down
to feed a furnace
with unfaithful
innocents

Visitors agree that besides the residue of the golden age, a vivid feeling of loss pervades in Andalusia, the scintillating sawdust of its making, side by side with the rubble of its demolition; the legacy of stonemasons, and the custom of engraving blessings for the future on the rim of wells, is therefore a poignant theme in the context of Al Andalus's destruction and erasure:

The Stonemason' Son Contemplates Death

Because my heart
became a kiln
I wished to die

The inscription on the tiles
made a prayer in butterfly script
crowning your well

May the water refresh your soul

The clanging of keys became loud
A soldier stood behind me pissing in the well

Someone sang in the distance
Couldn't tell if she was a Jew
Christian or Muslim

It was a devotional song

Al Andalus, once amorphous, not unlike Pakistan, a question mark filled in its earliest phase with gestures from the past, was cranked into becoming a golden age, not by force of ideology but by inspired hard work, reconfiguring tradition in the most spectacular ways. To praise Al Andalus is to praise not just possibility and vision, but a work ethic. Many poems in my book will honor and celebrate the collaborative, imaginative, accomplished work that Al Andalus is known for — work that prevailed against conflict and war. I will complete my book during a time of severe global tensions between Muslims and the West; a time of war and growing intolerance, fed by a shockingly rampant anti-intellectualism. I will watch, along with others, our collective fabric shredded into flags and shrouds, and will long for the bygone musk of books, reach for that Damascene hairpin bookmark.

The End of the War

> I entered the city gates in a blindfold
> led by nothing
> but the summer drift
> of fairy-roses
> the secret musk of books
>
> How the market puffed up
> with flags and shrouds
>
> For a few drachmas
> I bought a shroud for my sword
> and buried it
> under the Bitter-Almond tree
>
> Next I bought a pail of azaleas
> a lamp
> and a saffron mantilla
>
> wrapped in which all night
> I watched ink
> silently make sparrows
> out of its dormant language
>
> Morning broke
> on the page I was reading
> And I let words fall
> into tightly woven nests
> And I let illumination
> be the song

Marigolds

Trauma has its own devastating orchestra, a cacophony of news reporters, screaming, hysterical wailing, breathless eyewitness accounts, jumbled prayers and sirens.

On the morning of December 16th, 2014, I hear this cacophony from Peshawar, eight thousand miles away, in California. There has been a massacre of school children, an attack by gunmen on the campus of Army Public School; the attack is one of the world's deadliest to date, killing 149, injuring many. The news media are flooded with images of the young victims— aged 8 to 18, and faces of anguished parents. As I see the photos, a hopelessly dark curtain falls and I cannot tell one day from the next. I remain distracted from grief for months.

The six gunmen are identified as foreign nationals and eventually killed by Pakistan Army's Special Services Group. The surviving hostages describe them by their voices since their faces are covered. The attackers speak different foreign languages; the bloodbath they intend to carry out doesn't require much communication. There are other words spoken and memorialized: words spoken by the teachers to their students, the students to one another, desperate words to protect and help which are later repeated by survivors. These are the final offerings of duty and love.

I wander through the days silently as if bearing a heavy load of voices. The phantoms of my own past have tunneled through trauma. The voice of a teacher, sacred and beloved, recalled on so many occasions in my life as a migrant, comes back now with an instruction to hide under the desk. I know this voice but not this instruction; it is a different time. Eyewitness accounts of the tragedy are chilling. *Pretend to be dead.*

The child who whispered this to his classmate, hiding under a desk, as bullets were fired, was killed, while his classmate, the eyewitness who followed his advice, survived. He survived, we survived but we struggle to feel alive, weighed down as we are by despair.

The Soviet-Afghan war decades ago returns with disturbing clarity; I cannot help hearing Peshawar's proximity and the terrorist attacks that began as a consequence of Pakistan's involvement in a proxy war. The scenes of the new tragedy bring back the corridors of my own school, the inflections and even the footfall of every teacher, I remember our uniform shoes, gray school blazers.

I see the frightening image of broken combs.

Walking numbly through the farmer's market one day, I see a shock of marigolds and I break down at the sight. I'm reminded of the eve of my wedding, my "*haldi*," ceremony, the day the family lavishes the bride with turmeric and cream and all manner of beauty treatments. Marigolds had been brought that day instead of roses and jasmines because Peshawar was going through a cold spell and marigolds were the only flowers to survive.

Hundred and Thirty Two Coffins

(For the young victims of Peshawar Attacks)

I've slipped into a hundred
and thirty-two coffins
with
You
of the full smile
You

scented with Eucalyptus
and Chinar
baby shampoo pencil peels
father's aftershave
You
for whom we had grown trees
for fruit and shade
not coffins

Partings: The Concussion Year

The ghost that lurks around the old Bombay Company book-shelf is the ghost of an elliptical future, trailing the past like a spectacular, burning, comet-tail. It is the wispy energy of my own half-dreamed, half-written book that hovers over the rows of books I use for research, mostly works of history and poetry. After a night of writing, I have finally met my deadline. The life-size mirror leaning in the corner shows a pale face, preoccupied with time; my work is to not forget the past, and to call to poetry what may be forgotten. I am now searching for a book for remembrance, a book by the American Sufi poet Daniel Abdal-Hayy Moore. I want to honor this poet whose work I consider a beacon and who is now saying his goodbyes, dying of cancer. I am flailing for time, mine, his, and ours as poets, especially as Muslim poets living through times of brutal daily deaths. Weeks from now, earthly time will stop for him, moments from now, time will slow down for me, indefinitely.

The bookshelf phantom is poised to make projectiles of trea-sured objects— a miniature Chinese cabinet and framed Turkish calligraphic art on an easel— heavy objects that will slide down and cause a mild concussion and prolonged head/neck trauma. I am stunned but remain conscious, suddenly feeling extreme fatigue. It is ironic that one of the objects is Turkish— I had met Daniel Abdal-Hayy Moore and his wife Malika at the Nazim Hikmet Poetry Festival where he and I were both awarded the Nazim Hikmet Poetry Prize, where I recognized kindred souls in both Daniel and his wife Ma-lika and found a reservoir of inspiration and made lifelong friends at the Turkish House in Cary, North Carolina. De-spite the shock of the accident, I feel the surge of a promise, a kind of reassurance.

Over the next weeks and months, I will go through several phases and manifestations of the head and neck trauma. I will wait it out, struggle to continue my daily duties and keep promises to loved ones— kids' sleepovers with cousins, cooking birthday treats, coaching for a science competition— I will strain to finish projects until the pain and fatigue take over; I will give up my goal of finishing my book by the summer. I will travel alone and with family, and come to know the din of airports as being trapped in a plastic bag or walking the edges of a strange, serrated nightmare. I will feel helpless. I will also be the recipient of serendipity: I will be visited by childhood memories in unexpected places such as the ABBA museum in Stockholm or the Nivea store in Hamburg, reminisce with Nomi; I will read poetry among old friends and make new ones in many American cities, most memorably in Chicago, with Rizwan Kadir as the chief host. I will drink tea in some of the most beautiful gardens and have some of the saddest thoughts of my life.

In the course of the year, the political climate will ignite more mistrust, hatred and violence by white supremacists, particularly towards Muslims. At a reading in Portland, with my beloved mentor Lisa Steinman among the audience, I'd suddenly feel overwhelmed, find myself saying on stage how utterly tired I am of having to publicly translate reality as an American Muslim, to speak as a perpetual other; I'll feel cut-off from family who neither understand my health challenges nor my challenges as a writer, go home feeling exhausted and abandoned. As someone who covets solitude, I will for once discover its frigid side. Unable to read or write for extended periods, I will have my first brush with hard core isolation— a lesson in humility that will teach me to breathe with intent. I will no longer take breath for granted, nor will I take the beach, a mile away, for granted; I will catch more sunsets in six months than my whole life. I will be thankful to have my parents' hands to picture as I suffer through a long, claustrophobic session of MRI scans. I will find comfort in my mother's voice on the phone and in chanting the ninety-nine names of God. I will discover gifts of health in nature on my weekly walks with Sabiha, my sister-in-law.

There are signs nesting in signs. In between episodes of panic attacks and nausea, I aim to be the finest listener, an artist of stillness who cultivates the patience to mend her own wings, and remains in no hurry to fly. Dr. Bilal Choudry, my Neurologist invites me to his home to attend a Sufi zikr led by the celebrated Rumi scholar Kabir Helminsky only days before the end of the concussion year; my attention is gently brought back to time, to letting go of time, and thereby of making what is allotted to me truly mine. I reflect on Daniel's Muslim name— Abdal-Hayy, one in service of the ever-living Divine, the timeless One.

In Swat Valley: A Girl and a Woman

The most astonishing memory of Swat valley that remains with me since my first visit as a child is the euphoria of the headstrong *Darya e Swat*, the luxuriously frothy river, like fresh milk churning and churning joyfully. That, and the first time I heard the pristine and full silence of wilderness, meandering along languorous brooks and spotting the smallest wild flowers I had ever seen. Like any child, scale impressed me: the mountains were the highest, the river the fastest, the silence of the trails the deepest I had yet experienced. If there was anything subtle I may have observed, the awe of scale and novelty eclipsed it completely.

Visiting Swat again, I try to recapture that spirit of childhood, setting the senses free as well as refining them with the subtlety that was beyond the capacity of my younger self, wrestling furiously against the disquiet and frustration Swat evokes due to recent political events. It strikes me that subtlety still eludes the perception of Swat as far as the global psyche goes, dominated as it is by narratives of scale: the most unsafe place in the world, the worst place for women and education, home of the youngest person to receive the Nobel prize etc.

Those of us who have witnessed the cranking of the war-machine in the dissemination of half-truths and falsehoods in print, on screen, in the manufacture of celebrity, must reclaim for ourselves our own eyes and ears, our faith in what we know to be the truth about the culture we come from—not easy when over-simplification and lies-by-omission become standard practice/perception and therefore the "truth," when subtlety is drowned out by sensationalism. The test came for me when I received a blurb request for a book of poems that was sympathetic to Malala and her cause while exposing ignorance of the full historical and political context of Malala's story; the author conflated sentiments in response to what was actually a brief period of Taliban-rule in a small area of Pakistan, with the entire country and culture, coming across as if girls have never had access to education in Pakistan. In my letter to the publisher who had requested remarks of praise for the book, I wrote that I respected the author's compassion and mastery of craft, but I could not endorse a work that perpetuated the falsehood (even if only by insinuation) that women in Pakistan are not allowed to go to school. As someone indebted to the learning received from my grandmothers, one of them a college professor, and from women mentors and teachers who were aware and proud of their Muslim heritage of women thinkers, I could not participate in supporting a book with a focus so myopic and misleading as to be itself contradictory to the idea of education as a source of broadening the mind. A work enacting the pigeonholing that education is supposed to train the mind against, was a betrayal of my values.

On the one hand, I feel pride in the person of Malala, her intelligence, courage, and vision, and on the other, anger at witnessing how her story has been appropriated and reduced for propaganda, her own words censored wherever they don't fit the agenda of justifying war without end. Is Malala a hero? Yes, she is. But so are numerous other young Pakistani women and men who have risked their lives for their principles in a very difficult time, who have begun movements for education and social justice, even given their lives (as Aitzaz Hasan and Mashal Khan did) fighting violent extremism, or being in the crossfire between terrorists and the war on terror.

Years ago, before coming to the United States as a college student, I accompanied my mother to Swat on a her documentary-making trip. She had recruited me as a translation voice-over; the interviewees in her film (about self-employed women) spoke Urdu or Pashto, the voice-over for her film, commissioned by UNICEF, was in English. I was a preoccupied teenager, not impressed by anything, quite used to giving my mother half-hearted help in her projects. On that trip in 1992, I met women who ran schools, tailoring shops, "tandoors" (where bread is baked and sold), and so on. I was aware of the struggles of both women and men in our third world country, and thanks to my mother's activism as well as my father's, I was especially aware of the challenges of underprivileged women. In all honesty, this interested me as little at the time as the scenic beauty of Swat I had been so taken in by as a child. The world was big and I was ready for an adventure of my own.

My latest trip is different. I want this place to speak to me as an old friend, to separate the grain from the chaff of my spirit, to remind me who I was before the burnout of grownup life, before the exhaustion of raising Muslim children in America, teaching them to have patience with a world that is suspicious of us merely for existing, to value culture but be wary of tribalism in a time when divisive rhetoric is gaining currency and tribalism and polarization are becoming the norm.

Revisiting Swat, I want to heal from our abrasions, to be in tune with the spirit of childhood for myself and my sons (who are now in college/middle-school), as we travel with their grandparents, aunts, uncles and cousins.

The lush panoramas of Swat valley are wide and generous, like a grandparent's embrace. Swat's civilization, 3000 years old, is richly varied, with an impressive history, as we learn from our visit to Swat museum, and its original name, "Suvastu" means "lunar light reflected in the river." Our nighttime visit to a restaurant by the river is beautiful, even on a moonless night, and the rainbow trout brings back happy memories, as does a sun-dappled waterfall. But my hunger for the contrary gifts of simplicity and subtlety is only satiated, when, on a hike, we chance upon a quaint building, made by a son in honor of his mother. An inscription in Pashto reads: *Masjid Razia: May the prayers offered in this mosque be a blessing on my mother's soul.* This mosque with a slanted roof and vibrant colors sits sweetly in the midst of rolling hills; there is nothing somber about this place of worship, its scale is irrelevant— it reminds me of a joyful girl, a contented spirit— an unforgettable gesture of a son's regard for his mother.

Shampooing

Hidden in rituals of grooming and caregiving are words spoken only when we're unguarded. These are the rare moments we're physically in the hands of an unconditional love whose touch stimulates a unique language based on trust, opening the chute of memory or mystery.

Massaging, a common sight as part of the family scene during my childhood yields such words. Sisters and girl-cousins oil, massage, comb and braid each other's hair, grandparents massage the babies in the family; the same babies massage their grandparents when they are older. The deepest, most treasurable conversations ensue: the person being massaged may suddenly recall a forgotten incident, a song fragment, a joke, an old story or a snippet of family history, or may enter a contemplative space, a different dimension of consciousness or of long-guarded secrets. When I read about Freud's couch and his free recall technique, I'm reminded of various massaging scenes involving our lawn chairs, rugs, floor cushions, the village *"charpais,"* those painted rope cots, even the convolutions of the grapevine I studied while reclining against my mother's knees, the indulgent winter sunshine, teacups, biscuits, and the scent of oranges, most of all— the distinct timbre of each family member.

A traditional scalp massage, often part of the weekly or monthly routine, is believed to be good for blood circulation and brain health, and for maintaining strong, beautiful hair. From reading books such as Claire Chambers's *Britain Through Muslim Eyes*, I'd learn that *"Champooi"* or *"champi"* (meaning "to press or knead"), the art of the scalp massage using special oils and herb infusions, is the origin of the word "shampoo," and was brought (in addition to the Turkish bath and other grooming and wellness treatments) to Europe by one Sake Dean Mahomed, a doctor and entrepreneur from the Indian subcontinent who set up a spa in Brighton, England, in the eighteenth century. About a thousand years earlier, soap had arrived in Europe via Muslim Spain, from Allepo, Syria; it was said to be crafted from the combination of sweet bay oil, olive oil, lye and water, then heat-processed and aged before use. Public baths, rituals and products for cleansing, strengthening, beautifying and relaxing the body became popular in parts of Europe due to cultural influences from the East, and have been evolving globally ever since.

I remember the talk of *"amla"* and *"ritha"* herbal concoctions, the scent of coconut, mustard, almond and olive oils, how mothers would fuss over their children's heads— to ensure that their boys grow up brainy and girls beautiful. I wanted to be both. I remember raw egg-white masks and shampoos from my childhood and how the fruity and floral smells lingered. As a mother myself I recall learning to carefully cradle the baby's head and neck, rolling up small washcloths for neck-support in the tub, checking the temperature of the water and giving a gentle massage while shampooing; Toweling and talking to the baby afterwards, as pure a delight as one can dream of.

When we meet our first baby, he is a sound on the Doppler: the galloping rhythm of a heart. On the monitor of the ultrasound machine, he's a triumphant silhouette, a freely roving form that has the ambrosia of the womb waters all to itself. Because his heart gallops, I conjure him as a mythic seahorse. The hippocampus, the part of the brain that navigates spatial memory among other things, is named after the Greek word "hippokampos," meaning seahorse, likely for its shape. The first image of my child in utero will enter my psyche as a promise of remembering places together.

I soothe my children when they are babies by rubbing oil on their temples and stroking their hair, singing and telling them stories of the far-off places of my childhood. Yaseen, with his long lashes and deep gaze, seems to listen intently to poems I recite in Urdu, to the Spanish guitar and to the soundtrack of *The Lion King*. A winter-baby, his thick hair reminds me of fairytale woods, reaffirming the possibility of reaching contemplative depths through the imagination. His eyes hold enough wonder to last me many lifetimes; he becomes my finest, most generous teacher. He watches my mouth when I speak and when he begins to coo I hear different shades of the "k" sound. One day he surprises us and his pediatrician by vocalizing *"qaf"* — one of the most unique sounds of Urdu. He opens my world to the many languages that exist with no dictionaries but love.

When Yousuf is born, I know he's been tuned in to all the conversation and music I've been sharing with his older brother, now two years old. Yousuf, with his hazel eyes and tufts of curly hair, is my golden one. Born earlier than expected, he's a small baby who communicates efficiently, establishing himself as a creature of habit and teaching me the beauty of precise rhythms. He loves nothing more than having his hair shampooed, which is highly unusual for a newborn. I'm struck by the serendipity of shampooing him daily: the routine involves opening the curtains to luscious treetops in early spring, singing a song or two, talking, a gentle head- massage that he utterly gives himself up to, the berry and violet scent of the shampoo, and the distant prattle of his brother who is being looked after by *khala*, my aunt who is visiting specially for that purpose.

And then there is the one who wears his heart on his sleeve, Yousha, my youngest one, six years apart from Yousuf, and everyone's darling. Braving a complicated delivery and born a Leo, my only summer baby, he has a mane of red hair. As an infant, Yousha loves grooming and dressing; he kicks in excitement as I try to get his feet into his onesie knowing he's getting ready to ride the stroller to bring his brothers home from school. His strong-willed nature is a reminder that astronomical possibilities are within reach, that passion reveals itself in mysterious measures and it's enough just to behold its spark. No matter how much I try to tame his hair, it remains tousled and fierce, catching the light of the afternoon sun as I rock him in the hammock. I call him my lion cub and share my wide-toothed comb with him.

As my baby boys grow older, the hands-on moments of grooming grow less and less but the shared words remain with us— some of these words, a gift from my elders in various places. When Yousha is six months old, I begin graduate school, and soon after graduating, get a job that requires travel. I miss the children, especially the little one who is only three at the time. I ask my husband if the baby misses me, if he has said anything. Nothing, for a day or two. On the third day, Yousha asks him: "Has she taken her comb with her?"

In my years of traveling for work, I get the rare, fleeting opportunity to be in my parents' world again— to eat at the family dining table and keep my combs and styling brushes in the drawer of my mother's dressing table. But when I sleep, my mind floats to a time zone twelve hours distant. *Hippocampus, the part of the brain that navigates spatial memory, is named after the Greek word "hippokampos," meaning seahorse.* Many seas away are the hearts that once galloped inside my womb; every night I awaken exactly at 2:30 am, when it is 2:30 pm in California and my children are walking home from school. Across nearly ten thousand miles and ahead in time by half a spin of the earth, I send them prayers of protection.

Spatial memory necessitates paying attention to the singular demands of a place. When we travel, I teach my children to be cognizant, also to dress for long journeys: they must be comfortable and dignified, ideally wearing a full-sleeved undershirt, a semi-formal layer and a warm layer. If they're tired or fussy, I rub a little cream on their hands or Eucalyptus lotion on the temples. As teenagers, my boys are singled out for extra screening because they are Muslims; the thought of rough handling and abrasive interrogation, submitting not only my loved ones' vulnerable bodies to armed authority but also their vulnerable psyches, is distressful. In such instances, the distance between us is only a few feet but the hostility and dread that fill it seem infinite. This airport scene of being touched with suspicion, being spoken to with suspicion, unravels that painstaking weave, the daily lessons of building trust. To my surprise, my children prove to be stronger and calmer in the face of discrimination than I could imagine; whom have they taken after? Glimmers of the courage of elders braving wars and displacement shine through them. The weave hasn't unraveled after all. Our homes, in lands old and new, of this century or the previous, have one thing in common: regular moments of surrender to the care of loving hands and a voice that will come back to comfort, instruct, amuse or encourage whenever needed— long after the touch is gone.

Combing Song

From lampblack and pulp of a city's map
A sculpted pigeon rising as emperor
Inked, alighting on a vacuous alpine lap
Song of many combs and a single mirror

A sculpted pigeon rising as emperor
returning with a copper nib, a tourmaline book
Song of many combs and a single mirror
Speculum of storms, echo, inner eye and hook

Returning with a copper nib, a tourmaline book
Translucent and warm as eternity's milk—
speculum of storms, echo, inner eye and hook
of memory, childhood's dusty mulberry and silk

Translucent and warm as eternity's milk—
Inked, alighting on a vacuous alpine lap
of memory, childhood's dusty mulberry and silk
from lampblack and pulp of a city's map

Acknowledgements

Much gratitude to artist, scholar, and writer Salma Caller for contributing her art. I treasure her dynamic, exquisite work and it is truly a privilege to share these pages with her.

I'm greatly honored that Julia Bouwsma deemed this manuscript prize-worthy. Honored, also, to have had some of the finest and most dearly loved authors read and comment on this work. Deepest thanks to Deema Shehabi, Ilya Kaminsky and Bapsi Sidhwa. I'm grateful for the warm support I've had over the years from Eleanor Wilner, Zareena Saeed, Lisa Steinman, Marilyn Hacker, Fady Joudah, Ansa Zafar, Ilona Yusuf, Muneeza Shamsie, Sandra Alcosser, Claire Chambers, Dr. Azra Raza, Ambassador Akbar Ahmed, Dr. Amjad Hussain, Chris Murray, Peter O'Neill, Nazmi Agil, Efe Duyan, Nurduran Daman, Ishmael Von Heidrick-Barnes, Karen Kenyon, Wenhsiu Hassan, Pat Hansen, Brandon Cesmat, and the many friends from my Peshawar days. I'm fortunate to work with Melissa Hassard of Sable Press— a gracious and sensitive publisher. Thanks to Daniel Krawiec for honoring the intention and integrity of the work while designing the cover and interior. Much love to my brother Zafaryab who has been cheering me on since I was a baby, and to my son Yaseen without whose attentiveness to me throughout the many phases of writing and editing, this book would not exist.

The Darwish and Sepehri quotes in the opening pages are translations of the original by Fady Joudah (*If I were Another*) and Kazim Ali/ Mohammad Mahallati (*The Oasis of Now*) respectively. Thanks to Poetic Matrix Press, publisher of *Baker of Tarifa* and *Kohl & Chalk*, and to Jacar Press, publisher of *Ghazal Cosmopolitan*, excerpts from which appear in this book.

Special thanks to Abbas Raza, the editor of *3 Quarks Daily* where many of these essays were first published. Thanks also to the editors of *The Journal of Postcolonial Writings (UK)*, *Pakistaniaat: A Journal of Pakistan Studies (US)*, *Poetry International*, *In the Shape of a Human Body I am Visiting the Earth*, *UniVerse :: A United Nations of Poetry*, *Knot Magazine*, *Life and Legends*, *The Daily Times (Pakistan)*, *Live Encounters (Ireland)*, *Women's Voices for Change*, *Naya Daur*, and *Typehouse Literary Magazine* where some of the poems and prose pieces in this book first appeared.

Finally, this book is itself a means to give thanks for the rare love that sustains my writing life.

Shadab Zeest

About the Author

Photo: Shameem Hashmi

Shadab Zeest Hashmi is a Pakistani-American poet and essayist whose books include *Kohl and Chalk*, *Baker of Tarifa* and *Ghazal Cosmopolitan*.

Zeest Hashmi has won awards for her publications, her poems have been translated into Spanish, Turkish, and Urdu, and have appeared in numerous anthologies and journals worldwide, most recently in McSweeney's *In the Shape of a Human Body I am Visiting the Earth*.

About the Artist

Salma Ahmad Caller is an Egyptian/British artist and art historian, who was born in Iraq and grew up in Nigeria and Saudi Arabia. She now lives in the UK. Salma's art practice involves creating an imagery of the narratives of body that have shaped her own body and identity across profound cultural divides. Her work is strongly visual but also incorporates text and sound works. It is an investigation of the painful and contradictory mythologies surrounding the female body, processes of exoticization, and the legacy of colonialism as a cross-generational transmission of ideas, traumas, bodies and misconceptions. Her art practice is informed by a Masters in Art History and Theory, having studied medicine, and teaching cross-cultural perspectives at Pitt Rivers Museum in Oxford.

Artist's Statement: Cover Art

I wanted to convey the complex feelings that arose for me whilst reading Comb, about Shadab and her rich memories that constantly embroider her present. Sometimes we feel we are an assemblage of memory fragments, just like the old photos, objects and possessions that somehow manage to escape the multiple clearouts as we travel from place to place. Certain memories become like those auratic objects, resonating and emitting voices, scents and touch from the past into our daily lives. They irrevocably entangle us with our past selves. Photographs were taken using a vintage Vidicon lens, and collages of objects, watercolour paper with ink drawing, pencil drawing, gold dust, a photograph of Shadab, an old map of Peshawar, and magazine cuttings.

CPSIA information can be obtained
at www.ICGtesting.com
Printed in the USA
LVHW101924141222
735237LV00002B/348